CW01084058

RAINBOW
STARGAZERS

BY JEFF PERKINS

Interviews courtesy of Rock's Backpages

 **ABSTRACT SOUNDS BOOKS LTD**

Abstract Sounds Books Ltd
Unit 207, Buspace Studios, Conlan Street, London W10 5AP
www.abstractsoundsbooks.com

© Abstract Sounds Books Ltd 2010

Published by Abstract Sounds Books Ltd
Licensed from Archive Media Publishing Ltd
ISBN: 978-0-9566039-3-7

DVD CREDITS

Rainbow:
Ritchie Blackmore, Graham Bonnet, Cozy Powell, Roger Glover, Don Airey, Bobby Rondinelli, Joe Lynn Turner, David Rosenthal, Chuck Burgi, Doogie White, John O'Reilly, Greg Smith, Paul Morris, Candice Night

Interviewees:
Ritchie Blackmore*, Ronnie James Dio*, Doogie White, Don Airey, Bob Daisley, Jon Lord, David Coverdale*

All film interviews are copyright Archive Media Publishing Ltd
Audio interviews conducted by Steve Rosen* and Jerry Bloom*

Musical Criticism:
Hugh Fielder, Bryan Josh, Heather Findlay, James Gambold, Neil Murray, Jerry Ewing, Bob Carruthers, Pip Williams, Rob Corich, Jerry Bloom

DVD Still Photography Courtesy of:
Redferns Music Picture Library

Camera Work
Gary Moore

Editor
James Fowler

Producer & Director
Bob Carruthers

BOOK CREDITS

Written by: Jeff Perkins © Archive Media Publishing Ltd
Interviews page 73-116: Courtesy of Rock's Backpages

Book Photography Credits
Pictorial Press - Pages 6, 11, 14, 19, 28, 34, 38, 43, 51, 53, 55, 56, 57, 59, 60, 62, 64, 72, 83, 88, 98, 102, 107, 111 Rex Features - Pages 24, 48, 54, 58, 61, 63, 78, 92
Wikimedia Commons - Page 114

CONTENTS

CHAPTER ONE

By April 1975, tensions and disagreements within Deep Purple had deteriorated to such an extent that Ritchie Blackmore's decision to quit the band came as little surprise. Looking back at this crucial point in the history of one of British rock music's greatest bands, the writing had been on the wall and there to see for some time. Clashes between members of bands are nothing new, of course, and when a band such as Deep Purple is gifted enough to include some of the most influential rock figures of the time, disputes over creativity and direction and clashes of ego, along with the constant strains of touring together, combine in an explosive and volatile cocktail. Explosive is a perfect way to sum up Deep Purple's history from its very inception to the increasingly public disintegration of the so-called Mark III line-up.

The band that had ignited the music world with the release of the 'Deep Purple In Rock' album back in June 1970 had continued to produce an incendiary brand of music propelled by the guitar genius of Ritchie Blackmore. When 'In Rock' arrived, it managed to shake the foundations of rock with tracks as shockingly powerful as 'Bloodsucker' and 'Flight Of The Rat'. The album itself opens with 'Speed King', not only a Purple classic but also a track that acts as a perfect illustration of what the band was about at that time in their history and gives a brief insight into the internal conflict that began to affect and erode Blackmore's desire to continue with such heavy rock. It also illustrates both his and Jon Lord's classical influences and interests. 'Speed King' starts with an assault on the senses from Ritchie's guitar before the subtlety of Jon Lord's keys introduce a brief classical section. Suddenly, Ian Gillan's vocals take over and launch us into an album that changed both the direction of the band and of rock music. Blackmore's classical inspirations can be traced back to the very beginning of Deep Purple, and short but significant glimpses of his enjoyment of and fascination with Renaissance music appear time and again throughout his career. To create room for such diversions, he would first have to destroy his position within Deep Purple and create his own platform where some of his alternative ideas could be developed.

Meanwhile, during his dramatic on-and-off involvement as Deep Purple guitarist, Ritchie Blackmore will forever hold a place in rock as the man who fired off some of music's most famous and instantly recognisable riffs. His phenomenal reputation is still upheld today, and he often and quite justifiably appears in the listings among rock history's greatest guitarists. He was never one to take an easy path in his approach, his speed and accuracy reaching staggering proportions. His other reputation, for perfectionism, began to create tensions within the band as he became increasingly disillusioned with the band's setup and ruthlessly critical of his fellow band members and crew. He had always appeared to be volatile, a fact that added to his overall mystique and to the excitement of watching him play in a live situation: you were never quite certain if he would finish the number, let alone the set, or whether he would turn his back on a band member or the audience itself or simply explode in a display of some of the best rock guitar playing you could ever hope to witness. Many occasions of onstage spats have been captured and witnessed, but it was the band's offstage relationships that created an atmosphere that was both desperate and often dangerous. Deep Purple had already undergone several line-up changes by the time Blackmore left; it was a trend that continued throughout his new band Rainbow, where changes in personnel became a frequent feature.

Deep Purple's development has been well documented, with the band coming together from late 1967 and into early 1968, changing their name from Roundabout and including in the line-up vocalist Rod Evans

and bass player Nick Semper along with Blackmore, Jon Lord (keyboards) and Ian Paice (drums). Jon Lord had first teamed up with Ritchie Blackmore at the tail end of 1967, and it was immediately apparent to both musicians that that the pair not only shared similar influences including classical music but also enjoyed a vast combined wealth of talent. Rod Evans had joined from The Maze along with drummer Ian Paice, while Semper had arrived via Johnny Kidd & The Pirates. They quickly set out on tour and in the studio, where the first three Purple albums appeared in rapid-fire succession. The single 'Hush', released in July 1968, reached the top five in the US charts. The first album, 'Shades of Deep Purple', announced the band's arrival with a mixture of styles, giving a taste of future Purple paths. Following from that early success, the second album, 'The Book of Taliesyn' released in October 1968, further developed the various themes of the first. On display here is a maze of musical styles complete with classical undertones that would become an integral part of the history of both Jon Lord and Ritchie Blackmore. However, Blackmore was also instrumental in pushing the band further into the heavier side of rock whilst creating room for the odd nod in the direction these early works hinted at. Quite clearly he could see that this was the natural direction that would propel Deep Purple into the highest possible company in rock music. Further single success followed with 'Kentucky Woman' and 'River Deep Mountain High', and suddenly the band had become a recognised name in the music industry.

The third album, simply entitled 'Deep Purple', proved to be somewhat of a watershed; it would be the last offering from the original line-up as the band took the shift in the direction that Blackmore had been suggesting. Semper and Evans both left to be replaced by vocalist Ian Gillan and bass player Roger Glover, both from Episode Six. In fact, the band had two line-ups for a while, with the Mark I version fulfilling live dates whilst the soon-to-be Mark II setup met in the studio. It was therefore inevitable that the final parting would leave a bad taste. The Mark II version (Ritchie Blackmore, Jon Lord, Ian Paice, Ian Gillan and Roger Glover) is often referred to as the classic line-up of the band. The revered status of this particular version of the line-up is probably because it came during a time when Purple was grabbing rock by its neck and strangling it, demanding a response. Ian Gillan was exactly the right vocalist to give the band their sought-after hard rock sound and arrived along with bass player Roger Glover, who would go on to criss-cross the Deep Purple, Elf, Gillan and Rainbow family trees with much distinction. Having elected to take on a harder edge, it seems strange that the group performed and recorded a classical and rock orchestral piece, 'Concerto for Group & Orchestra', live at London's Royal Albert Hall in September 1969 and then moved to the studio, in an apparent tangent, to commence work on 'Deep Purple in Rock', their heaviest album to date by a long shot. Such was the array of talent that the band could have taken either musical direction, but of course it was their own particular brand of rock that led Deep Purple towards greatness. The single 'Black Night', strangely similar in name to Blackmore's current Renaissance group Blackmore's Night, had reached number two in the UK singles chart shortly after the release of 'In Rock'.

This period produced some of rock's most enduring classics, with the next two albums, 'Fireball' in October 1971 and 'Machine Head' in May 1972, both hitting the number one position on the album charts. Touring, writing, recording and appearances continued unabated, and a relentless schedule started to take its toll on both the health of the band and the relationships within it. Shortly after 'Live In Japan', arguably one of the greatest live albums ever and one that fully captured the power of Deep Purple in their prime, was released, Ian Gillan suddenly announced that he was leaving. Seemingly his relationship with Ritchie Blackmore had reached the breaking point, and at this point, the two musicians hardly exchanged a word between them. Just as the band could have and should have been building on the mammoth successes already achieved, it was quickly running the risk of imploding. The shock waves rebounded around the rock world as Purple began to try to find a replacement vocalist. It was no easy task as Ian Gillan's voice had become synonymous with everything Deep Purple.

During this process, in March 1973, 'Who Do You Think We Are' was released. The Mark II line-up had come to a rather acrimonious end, and Blackmore was beginning to develop yet another direction for the band: one that included a dual vocal style. The band brought in Glenn Hughes, ex Trapeze, to cover vocals. Hughes possessed a superb blues voice and fitted Blackmore's ideas perfectly, but he also played bass; as a result, Roger Glover found that his position within the band had become unworkable. However, Blackmore's and Glover's paths were destined to cross once again in the future. Paul Rogers of Free and Bad Company was a possible recruit to Deep Purple Mark III, but it was the previously unknown 22-year-old David Coverdale who took the position, turning in an audition that left the band, particularly Ritchie Blackmore, with no doubt that this was the man to team up with Glenn Hughes on vocals and become the band's new front man. During this time Blackmore and Ian Paice had been discussing the possibility of working together away from Deep Purple, but as it transpired, it would be several more years down the line and into the Rainbow era before this would finally come about. Despite some early trepidation, Coverdale proved to be a worthy choice, and the first release by the new line-up of Blackmore, Lord, Paice, Hughes and Coverdale, the album 'Burn', put to rest any lingering doubts with a solid bluesy and funky approach that still maintained the now expected power of the band. It sold quickly and contained some new Purple classics such as the title track and 'Mistreated'. When the band appeared live with Ritchie Blackmore's power-driven version of 'Burn', it was clear that despite the disappointment over the way that the Mark II line-up had ended, Deep Purple had maintained their standing in the rock world.

In December 1974 the album 'Stormbringer' arrived with a further development of the Glenn Hughes inspired funk and soul style, and it was at this point that Ritchie Blackmore's tenure in the band began to look decidedly shaky. Familiar tensions and disagreements developed, and upon the album's release, Blackmore finally began to develop a band away from Purple. It would be a band that would allow room for his musical ideas and space for his own development, away from his increasing disillusionment with Deep Purple. In early 1975, he invited the band Elf, who had been recently supporting Deep Purple, to join him, and from that collaboration Ritchie Blackmore's Rainbow was born. Rainbow would go on to provide an essential outlet for Blackmore's talents through an output of nine studio albums and several live releases along with the chance to team up once again with both Ian Paice and Roger Glover along the way. All the essential Blackmore traits are apparent in the early Rainbow recordings, and the classical and Renaissance foundations of many of the tracks illustrate his growing desire to go his own way from the direction that Deep Purple had gone.

This was a process that ultimately resulted in the creation of Blackmore's Night, a full-on Renaissance experience, a band that has created surprise, shock and a lot of misunderstanding particularly in the rock media over his apparent 'loss' to rock. It has to be pointed out that Ritchie Blackmore has left a rich and lengthy legacy of over 40 years of some of the best rock guitar available with both Deep Purple and Rainbow and that if he chooses to take another turn away from rock and into a field of music that has clearly inspired him throughout that career, then who can criticise that decision? In true Blackmore tradition he applies himself totally to his new muse and his musicianship, as ever, cannot be criticised. When he left to form Rainbow, a return to Deep Purple looked highly unlikely, but as the saying goes, 'never say never'; this is particularly true with Ritchie Blackmore. He is, after all, very much his own man and follows his own paths in music. His considerable track record and reputation have of course allowed him to do this; as a result, we now have a catalogue of eclectic music from one end of the spectrum to another. There are not many rock guitarists who can claim that achievement. The fact that he is no longer standing on stage firing out 'Smoke On The Water' is a shame, but he is performing music that is equally enjoyed, albeit in a different genre and by a different audience.

Blackmore rejoined Purple in 1984, having put Rainbow temporarily on hold, and in so doing found himself in an unlikely Deep Purple Mark II reunion, complete with Ian Gillan and a renewal of their sometimes troubled relationship. Deep Purple had derailed back in 1976 alongside familiar squabbles and growing drug problems within the band. Brilliant guitarist Tommy Bolin would, sadly, succumb to his heroin addiction in December 1976, and meanwhile Glenn Hughes had also been fighting his own demons. David Coverdale had gone on to form the hugely successful Whitesnake, and Ritchie Blackmore's Rainbow and Ian Gillan's 'Gillan' band had all helped keep the Purple legacy well and truly in the public consciousness.

When the Mark II reunion was officially announced, it caused wide scale excitement among an eager rock world, most of whom had never been fortunate enough to see the 'classic' Purple line-up perform. The first offering was the album 'Perfect Strangers', released in November 1984, and that was quickly followed up with tour dates as the album rose to number five in the UK album listings. In January 1987 the 'House Of Blue Light' album appeared to largely mixed reviews. In many respects the band's essential sound was still evident, but each member had been on a journey away from Purple and the result is a sometimes uncomfortable mixture that, not surprisingly, fails to achieve the levels of past glories. This was illustrated with the next Mark II album 'Nobody's Perfect', a live album that highlighted the power of older, more familiar Purple classics. In true Deep Purple tradition, particularly in relation to this line-up, the reunion had to end in tears. In 1988, following more problems between the singer and Blackmore over some of his performances, Ian Gillan branched off to work on a joint album project with Roger Glover entitled 'Accidentally on Purpose'. He stayed behind when Deep Purple got back together to write and rehearse new material in the States, and the end came when he was fired from the band the following year. After many months of trying out replacement vocalists, it was Ritchie Blackmore who was influential in the choice of Joe Lynn Turner as the new singer. Joe had been with Ritchie's Rainbow and could cover the more melodic sound that Blackmore now sought for Purple. This was the Mark V version of Deep Purple—Blackmore, Lord, Paice, Glover and Joe Lynn Turner—and the album 'Slaves and Masters' resulted. It was a clear move towards AOR (Album Oriented Rock) and was received with mixed reviews mainly stating that it did not feel like a Purple album.

Ian Paice, Roger Glover and Jon Lord were quickly growing tired of this new direction and approached Ian Gillan to once again try and bury the previous ill feeling and rejoin. Joe Lynn Turner was dispensed with, and late in 1992, Gillan returned in a wave of media excitement. The album that came from this latest reincarnation of the classic Mark II line-up was called, rather appropriately, 'The Battle Rages on' and, of course, to a large extent it did. The album was strongly influenced by Ian Gillan, who was seemingly less

Photo: Pictorial Press

inclined to take a back seat and pushed for a heavier sound more akin to the Mark II of old. It opens with the superbly Purplesque title track that more than hinted at what could follow if the internal problems could be laid to rest. Despite the personality conflicts, the album gave Blackmore the opportunity to come up with some storming riffs once again. When the band played live, they somehow managed to push the ever-present tension into their personal performances, and Blackmore in particular turned in some of his most remarkable solos as a result. Once again the end loomed when Blackmore fell out with an onstage camera crew, throwing a glass of liquid at them before finally leaving Deep Purple for the last time in 1993. He returned to the Rainbow project and produced their last album before going Medieval. Deep Purple have remained reasonably constant since his departure and have enjoyed something of a renaissance of their own with Steve Morse filling the guitar slot and Don Airey, of Rainbow, replacing Jon Lord, who has retired from live performances. They have released new albums such as 2003's disappointing 'Bananas' and the much superior 2006 'Rapture of the Deep'.

This, then, is the ever-changing background of the founder of the band Rainbow and illustrates how intrinsically linked by the respective family trees Deep Purple, Rainbow, Gillan and Whitesnake are. It was with his band Rainbow that Ritchie Blackmore finally had total control, and as a direct result the band created an impressive array of rock music including some interesting and varied diversions and experiments along the way. Just as with Deep Purple, Rainbow would experience numerous changes in personnel throughout its life, resulting in a total of over 20 different musicians involved with the band. It is a story of commercial highs and disappointing lows, quality musicianship and the occasional strange decision that helps to illustrate some of the complexity of the character of its leader. There were several turns in directions, wholesale band changes and stadium-sized success, as impressive album and single sales resulted in major airplay, all of which helped propel Rainbow to the top. Having taken his band to this point, he suddenly made an unlikely return to Deep Purple, putting a temporary hold on Rainbow activity. Once the Mark II Purple reunion had run its inevitable course, Blackmore briefly reunited Rainbow before finally following his muse and musical instincts in creating Blackmore's Night.

Whatever has been said or written about him, Ritchie Blackmore has carved out several unique paths whilst remaining a true rock guitar hero. Quite often misrepresented, misunderstood and possibly, excuse the pun, mistreated, he remains very much his own man. Once released from the conflict that Deep Purple had become, he was suddenly free to pursue his own paths and musical goals. Rainbow was created at exactly the right time for him, and he was now able to take this band in whatever direction he chose. The history of this band can therefore also be seen as a glimpse into the mind of one of the most charismatic and yet unpredictable rock heroes of all time. This is a critical review of Rainbow and one of the greatest guitarists the world has ever seen.

CHAPTER TWO

The sense of inevitability regarding Ritchie Blackmore's departure from Deep Purple did little to quell the great dismay felt by countless fans of the band once it finally happened. The constant disagreements within the group had convinced him that the only way to carve out a route for his own musical direction would be by creating his own band that would act under his leadership and control. Within such a setup, he would not have to seek the approval and agreement of others in situations that had caused so much discord in the past. Whilst the remaining members of Deep Purple went about the unenviable task of trying to fill the huge gap on guitar that his departure had left, Ritchie was hatching plans to go it alone. Inspired by what he had seen and heard of them, he turned to Deep Purple's recent support band Elf to provide the basis of his new venture.

In fact the whole of Deep Purple had been very impressed with Elf, to such an extent that Roger Glover and Ian Paice, who had witnessed their audition for Columbia in 1972, not only invited them to support them on tour but also offered to co-produce an album for them. During the tour, Elf continued to attract favourable reviews, and Blackmore began to see them as an ideal, ready-made unit within which he could position his full range of guitar genius. He began to be seen together with Elf's lead singer, one Ronnie James Dio, and plans for the creation of the new band began to take shape. When, during the 'Stormbringer' sessions in late 1974, the other members of Deep Purple firmly vetoed Blackmore's suggestion that they cover the 1970 Quatermass track 'Black Sheep Of The Family', he decided to go into the studio along with members of Elf and record it anyway. The single sold well and the b-side, which had been written along with Ronnie James Dio, proved that there was potential mileage in this collaboration. He decided to go ahead and produce an album with Elf. He would then complete the adoption by absorbing Elf under the banner of his new band's name. One of their favourite haunts was a nightclub in Los Angeles, California named The Rainbow, a regular stop for the passing rock circus of the day. It was during a typical all-day session in The Rainbow that Ritchie and Ronnie James Dio decided to form a band and name it after their favourite place. As accomplished and exciting a singer as Dio undoubtedly was, the chance to join forces with Blackmore and all the media attention that such a venture would bring proved irresistible. Elf was, sadly, shelved and Ritchie Blackmore's Rainbow was born.

Elf had already achieved an impressive following, and their first album 'Elf', released in 1972, introduced a band displaying plenty of potential. Further Roger Glover-produced albums attracted further interest in the band, but it was the performances of their diminutive lead singer that really captured the imagination. Ronnie James Dio had been born to a family of Italian heritage as Ronald James Padavona in New Hampshire in 1942, although this date is open to some conjecture with Ronnie himself sometimes claiming to having been born as late as 1949. His first recorded work appeared back in 1958 when the very young Dio could be heard fronting a rockabilly band called The Vegas Kings. In 1961 he was singing with Ronnie and The Rumblers and then Ronnie and The Red Caps, and by the mid-sixties he was leading a band called Ronnie Dio and The Prophets. This band was followed by The Electric Elves, a forerunner of Elf, who featured the future Mötley Crüe manager Doug Thaler on keyboards. The Electric Elves became The Elves, and finally, at the tail end of the sixties, Elf was formed. Elf was essentially a blues-rock band performing material that gave Dio the perfect opportunity to display his impressive vocal talent that would later front such bands as Rainbow, Black Sabbath and his own band Dio. Elf originally consisted of the previously mentioned

Doug Thaler on keys and guitar, Nick Pantas's lead guitar, Gary Driscoll on drums and, of course, front man Dio himself, who also filled in on bass. Tragedy struck the band in 1970 when a car crash involving the band claimed the life of Nick Pantas and seriously injured Thaler, who subsequently quit the band. Pantas's death robbed the band of the searing blues of his guitar and the music world of a guitarist of immense promise. It has a hard blow, but Elf continued, recruiting Dio's cousin Dave Feinstein to take the guitar slot. Doug Thaler was later replaced by keyboard player Mickey Lee Soule. Soule had recently served time in the United States army and joined Elf on his release. Drummer Driscoll had graduated through the American R&B scene, playing with several bands until his recruitment into The Electric Elves. His story is also one that ended in tragedy: long after his departure from Rainbow and having played with Dakota and Bible Black among others, he was found brutally murdered in his home in Ithaca in New York State in 1987. It was a shockingly violent death and the motive behind it remains a mystery. He was only 41 years old.

The introduction of Mickey Lee Soule's keyboards helped turn their first album, the self-titled 'Elf' recorded in Atlanta, Georgia, released in 1972 and produced by Purple's Roger Glover and Ian Paice, into something of a treat. This album, with its tracks such as the searing blues of 'First Avenue', a track that includes superb Soule blues keyboards and is led by the irrepressible Dio's vocals, can be seen as a lost gem. The band had knitted together superbly by this time, and the impressive blues guitar of Dave Feinstein, later of The Rods, Soule's keys and Dio's huge voice combine to produce other quality tracks such as 'Hoochie Koochie Lady', the perfect vehicle for Mickey Lee, and a track that includes a superb solo by Dave Feinstein, a combination repeated to great effect on another track called 'Love Me Like a Woman'. 'I'm Coming Back For You' is typical of the era and could have been written by a number of bands but is delivered with Dio powering the vocals to such an extent that it turns what could have been an average track into something altogether more memorable. Elf is an all-round strong first album, and despite being lost in the subsequent shadow of Rainbow, is well worth revisiting.

By the time Elf's second album arrived, Dave Feinstein had left, taking his quite considerable talent to form The Rods and produce a first album on which his huge potential took off. Despite a lengthy time away from rock music, he has subsequently become one of the most respected and admired of rock guitarists and has now fully earned the pseudonym of Dave 'Rock' Feinstein. He was replaced by Steve Edwards when Elf also recruited bass player Craig Gruber, thereby releasing Dio to become an all-out front man for the band. After Elf/Rainbow Gruber would go on to play with Gary Moore on the 'Victim Of The Future' tour along with Purple's Ian Paice and to appear with Black Sabbath. With producer Roger Glover again on board, the 1974 album 'Carolina County Ball' (a.k.a. 'L.A. 59' in the States and Japan) is Elf at its very best in their all-too-short but dramatic history. Once again they opened for Purple, and with performances that could not fail to impress, again caught the eye and ears of Ritchie Blackmore. In Steve Edwards they had found a more than adequate replacement for Feinstein, witness his guitar solo on 'Annie New Orleans'. Other stand-out tracks from 'Carolina County Ball' are 'Ain't It All Amusing', a real classic rock track, 'L.A. 59' a track that once again featured Micky Lee Soule's fantastic keyboards and 'Do The Same Thing' a track that highlights the growing authority of Ronnie James Dio's vocal delivery. Included on the album is a taste of things to come with a track called 'Rainbow', one of the highlights amongst an impressive set of songs. The last song in the set, 'Blanche', is perhaps the only disappointment, resting rather uncomfortably in an otherwise superbly strong album. Elf had found and developed their sound quickly and decisively. History would have it that only one more album, 1975's 'Trying To Burn The Sun' which now included Mark Nauseef, later of The Ian Gillan Band and thereby establishing yet another Elf/Deep Purple connection, would be released. By the time it came out, the absorption of Elf into Ritchie Blackmore's Rainbow had all but ended the band. In its brief time span, Elf had caused quite a stir among the Deep Purple camp, and such was their growing relationship with Deep Purple that they also appeared as guests on Roger Glover's solo album 'The Butterfly Ball and The Grasshopper Feast'. It is no surprise, then, that when Blackmore decided to move away from Purple and into his own project, he approached Elf's Dio, and a new instant band was formed. Also unsurprisingly, it was guitarist Steve Edwards who moved out as Elf became Ritchie Blackmore's Rainbow.

Ritchie Blackmore's Rainbow was finally announced to the music world in May 1975 with an initial line-up of Blackmore on lead, Dio on vocals, Gruber on bass, Mickey Lee Soule on keys and Gary Driscoll on drums. An early interview with Ronnie James Dio and Ritchie Blackmore on 'The Rainbow Radio Special 1975' (and produced here with acknowledgement to the excellent Rainbow Fan Clan web site) confirms the similarity of both Rainbow founders' musical influences and gives a clear insight into Blackmore's ultimate musical direction when he says of the first album, 'When we formed Rainbow, Ronnie and I had the same interest in music which were basically Medieval classical roots such as Bach. Actually the whole L.P. was inspired by Johann, who was there some of the time, and a lot of progressions we used were classical progressions. That's not as drastic as it sounds; they're still rock progressions because I believe that Bach even in the 16th Century was still playing in a way that was very relative to the way that people are playing today.

Which is very rhythmical and we both had the same interest, so we tried to incorporate these Medieval parts. We used a lot of modes instead of scales, and modes meant we used weird chords, but we found that it worked with a rock backing. We achieved this on about four tracks and I'm very excited about it because I have never done this before, and it turned out very well'. He goes on to add, rather interestingly when considering the later formation of Blackmore's Night, 'Why I am so interested in Medieval stuff is because my hobby is psychic research and I believe in the supernatural and reincarnation. It creeps in and I think that I was around in maybe the 16th Century'.

Either way, Blackmore had indeed been around a while and his influence on rock music whilst with Deep Purple had been burned into our musical consciousness with riffs as endurable as 'Smoke On The Water' and 'Black Night', but here he was about to embark on a whole new project. The rock music world eagerly awaited the first offering from the newly formed Rainbow. Ritchie Blackmore's Rainbow was up and running.

19

CHAPTER THREE

From February 20th to March 14th 1975, Rainbow disappeared into the Musicland Studios in Munich, Germany. Blackmore finally announced his decision to leave Deep Purple during the following month, April, and despite the news being feared by the fans, it really came as little surprise to anyone. However, the exciting news of the new band went some way to alleviating the disappointment of the prospect of a Blackmore-less Deep Purple whilst providing the rock media with plenty of fodder to discuss what the future held for both bands. Whilst Purple held auditions that finally resulted in the mercurial but ultimately doomed Tommy Bolin moving into the band, Blackmore was working on Rainbow's debut album.

The album was produced by Blackmore, Dio and Martin Birch and lists among the credits J.S. Bach. Mixing was also undertaken by Birch, one of the all-time great producers, who can list Whitesnake, Black Sabbath, Deep Purple, Fleetwood Mac, Iron Maiden, Blue Oyster Cult and The Faces among his impressive credits, and all songs, with the exception of a re-working of The Yardbirds classic 'Still I'm Sad', were credited to Blackmore and Dio with the vocalist also claiming the lyrics. The excitement of finally holding the gatefold vinyl on its release is something I can still sense today. The cover, designed by David Willardson, depicts a dark and mysterious castle with Blackmore's Fender arm soaring from its centre into a rainbow across the sky. The centre spread is a superb collection of classic black-and-white photographs by legendary rock photographer Fin Costello. It was eye-catching and colourful, and the album inside proved to be much the same.

Opening with the soon-to-be Rainbow classic 'Man On The Silver Mountain' it was an album that underlined the intention, promise and the incendiary combination of Dio and Blackmore. It is the perfect opener for not only the album but for Rainbow as a band, announcing their arrival with a stunningly effective track that contains all the essential elements: a superb riff and stunning solo by Blackmore and the by now trademark power vocals by Dio. It remained an automatic choice for all subsequent versions of Rainbow when on tour and always features in top listings by Rainbow followers. The lyrics come from the pen of Dio and certainly set the scene for what the Rainbow project was all about. It has also stood the test of time to great effect as well and still sounds fresh. As for the guitar, it is a deceptively difficult riff to reproduce and in true Blackmore style never follows the easy path. This section is so typical, if you can say that about him, being technical, incredibly clean and effective: it once again illustrates the genius of the guitar playing side of the man. Second up is 'Self Portrait'. Opening with another quality riff, it's a slower, steadier and altogether darker track that still contains the essential, unmistakable Blackmore touch of genius. By this time the album is well under way with two quality tracks leading to 'Black Sheep Of The Family'. This was the track that Blackmore had been compelled to break away from Purple to cover and in truth, the result is a standard rock track that could have been worked by any number of bands but leads smoothly into one of the album's highlights, 'Catch The Rainbow', a wonderfully constructed melodic piece with an opening sequence that is more than a touch reminiscent of Jimi Hendrix. It provides a haunting track and allows Dio to show he can deliver a song sensitively whilst providing the band with guaranteed late-night airplay that quite probably assisted the album to rise to number 30 in the US charts. It remains a true Rainbow classic.

'Snake Charmer' opens side two (for those who can remember the days of vinyl) and opens another door in the Dio repertoire with a powerful delivery of an otherwise potentially standard track. It is tight and predictable but contains yet another superbly executed Blackmore solo and break built upon the tightest bass and drums that you could hope to hear. It is at the point when 'Temple Of The King's seductive opening chords lead you in that you realise what a well-constructed and balanced album this is. This hauntingly effective acoustic track fits perfectly within the whole and is expertly positioned within the set for maximum effect. From here the album moves into its final phase with the typically Elf 'If You Don't Like Rock And Roll', another standard rocker with a trademark piano solo from the former band's Mickey Lee-Soule before that gives way to the curiously named 'Sixteenth Century Greensleeves'. This is a track that maintains the quality and pedigree of the album as a whole, freshened by another Blackmore solo and some inspired Medieval lyrics. For anyone wondering what Blackmore is up to now with his Blackmore's Night incarnation, the clues are surely all here on this album. It all ends with a lovely piece of Blackmore covering a track from The Yardbirds, a band that boasted Jimmy Page, Eric Clapton and Jeff Beck within its remarkable history, the evergreen 'Still I'm Sad' in almost Hank Marvin Shadows style. It is an opportunity for him, as if he needed it, to showcase his guitar skills and his seemingly effortless repertoire. More importantly, it once again highlights his fascination with music from the past. 'Still I'm Sad', as both Blackmore and Dio were keen to point out, is based upon a Gregorian chant sequence that had been picked up and re-worked by The Yardbirds. It dates from the thirteenth century, and its choice on the very first Rainbow album was not only brave but gave all new Rainbow followers and latter-day Blackmore scholars a glimpse of what music really motivated this man.

The album caused a stir and set Rainbow on a road to wherever Blackmore chose to take them. It was to be a road that would ultimately highlight his many, but by now typical, changes in direction littered with ruthless band changes and a road that, despite the band becoming huge venue fillers, was equally marred by apparent indecision and near confusion. After all the fuss and suspense, the album clocked in at little over 37 minutes, but it set the scene for what Rainbow wanted to be, and it wouldn't be long before the band had dramatically changed with the course set for the second album 'Rainbow Rising'. In true Blackmore style, the remaining members of Elf were dismissed as his doubts about their suitability to undertake a Rainbow tour grew. In July 1975 Craig Gruber, Mickey Lee-Soule and Gary Driscoll all left and were replaced by Tony Carey on keyboards, Jimmy Bain on bass and the legendary Cozy Powell on drums. Despite the almost cruel death of the remnants of Elf, no one can argue over the quality of this new line-up, and once together it would prove to be the one that propelled Rainbow to the very top.

Jimmy Bain, born in the Scottish Highlands before emigrating with his parents to Vancouver, Canada, joined Rainbow from Harlot, a band that Blackmore had been impressed with when he saw them play London's Marquee. His early career had been with a band called Street Noise, and before responding to Blackmore's call, Bain had turned down a job with The Babys. Unfortunately, his tenure within Rainbow was destined, like so many others, to be short-lived. He appeared on the Rainbow Rising album and completed a world tour with them, but was subsequently sacked in January 1977 to be briefly replaced by Mark Clarke. After Rainbow he subsequently worked with such rock visionaries as Ian Hunter and John Cale before teaming up with ex-Thin Lizzy guitarist Brian Robertson to form Wild Horses, who released two albums, before going on to work with Roy Harper, Roger Chapman (ex-Family), Iron Maiden's Bruce Dickinson, Kate Bush and Gary Moore. He also met and worked alongside Phil Lynott, helping him to write material for his post-Lizzy solo albums and touring with him playing keyboards as the bass was obviously more than adequately covered. Later he rejoined his former Rainbow colleague Dio in a move that once again gave him the chance to co-write, which can be heard to good effect on the singer's solo concept albums 'Magica' and 'Killing The Dragon'.

Keyboard player Tony Carey, recruited at the same time as Bain but some six years younger, had been spotted by Blackmore whilst covering keys for the band Blessings. Tony was destined to remain in Rainbow on and off for two years before he became the latest member to be removed. After his departure from Rainbow, during which he appeared on 'Rainbow Rising' and 'On Stage', Carey's career took many twists and turns. First, along with producer Peter Hauke, he released solo material before forming the band Planet P Project. He has also become a respected producer in his own right and has worked with Eric Burdon, John Mayall and Joe Cocker amongst others. In 1984 he scored a success with 'A Fine, Fine Day' and 'I Won't Be Home Tonight'.

English drummer Cozy Powell, born Colin Flooks, had already built up a massive reputation before attending the Los Angeles audition for the newly vacant drummer's spot in Rainbow. Cozy had started his career with the Sorcerers back in the mid-sixties before teaming with ex-Yardbird Jeff Beck for two albums. His solo record 'Dance With The Devil' had reached the top three in the UK charts in 1973, and he had also been involved with his own band Bedlam. Further single successes followed for him as part of Cozy Powell's Hammer, a band that included one Bernie Marsden, of UFO and later of Whitesnake fame. Joining Rainbow in 1975 gave him the ideal platform to perform regularly at arena-sized events, where his speed and dramatic

playing enhanced his already considerable name. He was to be a relative Rainbow survivor, staying the course before bowing out after the first Monsters Of Rock festival in August 1980. Cozy then began work on a solo album called 'Tilt' which was released before he joined the Michael Schenker Group in 1981 and ex-Deep Purple David Coverdale's Whitesnake from 1982 to 1984 before working with Keith Emerson and Greg Lake in 1986, Gary Moore in 1989 and on and off with Black Sabbath until 1995, when he got together with Brain May for two albums. His life ended tragically when on 5 April 1998 his Saab 9000 crashed on the M4 motorway near Bristol, but he left a legacy of over 60 appearances on major rock albums and is widely regarded as one of the most respected rock drummers in history.

In November 1975, the new Rainbow line-up of Blackmore, Dio, Bain, Powell and Carey took to the road starting in America. It was a spectacular line-up, and the quality of musicianship could not be doubted. Jimmy Bain and Cozy Powell linked well, driving the band whilst releasing Blackmore to express himself superbly on guitar. All this was fronted, of course, by the dynamic Dio and backed smoothly by the keyboards of Tony Carey. The band played material from the first album underneath a huge electronic rainbow that spanned the stage. By February 1976, they had written enough material for the band's second album. They returned to the Musicland Studios in Munich and recorded 'Rainbow Rising' over a 10-day period. It was an album that was once again superbly produced by Martin Birch. The double gatefold cover, painted by Ken Kelly, depicts a huge fist gripping a rainbow rising from the sea below. The castle from the first album cover remains and a soldier looks on at the dramatic scene from the rocks. The album's photography, which includes live shots and a central group study, was once again undertaken by Fin Costello. This is the album that confirmed Rainbow's status in the rock world and further explored the classical and medieval themes that had been heard on the first album.

The album was written once again by the Blackmore and Dio combination and opens with all the sense of drama and suspense that the first album left wafting on the air with 'Tarot Woman'. The track opens with Tony Carey's hauntingly effective keyboards leading into the inevitable, breathtaking arrival of Ritchie Blackmore. Dio, as ever, gives a wholehearted and powerful delivery that lifts the track even higher, helping to create a stunning opener that grabs the attention from the off. 'Run With The Wolf', the second track, continues in much the same vein and provides an opportunity to listen to the driving force behind the band, drummer Cozy Powell. Already there is no doubt that this album is a heavier and more solid album than the first, and Martin Birch's production fully captures the power and drama that is unfolding. 'Starstruck', followed by 'Do You Close Your Eyes', both open as more standard and slightly predictable rockers that perfectly display all of Rainbow's strengths at the time. Solid, driving and incredibly powerful, they are built on the most solid of foundations allowing Blackmore the space he often craved with Purple. These tracks close side one of the vinyl album and do not give any hint of what was ahead when the listener turned over for the incredible epic 'Stargazer'.

This is a track that contains all the dramatic and evocative visual imagery of Dio's lyrics with the 'shadow of the wizard', 'towers of stone', 'whips and chains' and 'blood in the sand' helping to conjure up a huge track that must rank among the highlights in all of Rainbow's subsequent career. There are some very similar Moroccan influences to those of Jimmy Page and Robert Plant's 'Kashmir', which appeared on the Led Zeppelin double album 'Physical Graffiti' exactly a year earlier in February 1975. 'Stargazer' is anthemic, colossal, breathtakingly massive in scale and is a Blackmore guitar highlight among so many other magical moments throughout a career that is so hard to fully define. It is a searing, soaring, stunning and masterful example of his incredible and instantly recognisable ability. This, combined with Dio's vocals complementing the nature of the song perfectly and Cozy Powell confirming his position among the drumming elite with a masterly performance, an orchestral backdrop and more atmosphere than is healthy for the average rock fan, it is a highlight not only for this album but for the era in rock itself. It is undoubtedly a Rainbow classic, with the very best musicianship from every member of the band, silencing the critics who had picked up on the shortness of the first album by delivering a mammoth, breathtaking masterpiece that would ultimately prove hard to better. The album finishes with 'A Light in The Black', a fast-moving return to some form of normality with Cozy's drumming once again underpinning the whole band as Jimmy Bain's bass takes some of the ex-Uriah Heep bassist Gary Thain-inspired walks. Tony Carey produces a keyboard solo that somehow defines the feel of the album, and when the second side closes and brings an end to Rainbow's second offering, it leaves the weighty impression that there must have been more material here. Such was the rich vein that the band had tapped into that a double album could have been possible, although it would have been a gamble to do that so early in the band's life. 'Rainbow Rising' was a triumph in most areas and the band, now complete with a more than impressive array of talent and reputations, was truly breaking ground with a distinctive writing style that utilised their many diverse influences.

It would be a hard act to follow as epic adventures such as 'Stargazer' are not easily repeated, and the ultimate lurch towards commercialism subsequently taken by Rainbow was, in retrospect, hardly a surprise.

The first world tour started in June 1976 and the band, with enough solid material from the two albums, produced a tour that was a great success both commercially and in building upon their growing fan base. Their first European appearances started at the end of August 1976 and were nearly all sell-outs before the band moved onto Australia and, familiar Blackmore territory, Japan towards the tail end of the year. In early 1977, there was another twist of Blackmore unpredictability when Jimmy Bain was sacked and was quickly followed out of the revolving Rainbow door by Tony Carey. Carey was soon re-hired to play with the band as a session musician, and Mark Clarke arrived to cover the bass. It is hard to understand why Bain was sacked after such a performance as 'Rainbow Rising'; the official line suggested that Blackmore had not found him to be fast enough, providing at least a partial answer. Tony Carey and newcomer Mark Clarke, meanwhile, didn't last long into the sessions for a new album. Carey left halfway through and Clarke was sacked, resulting in Blackmore covering some bass parts.

Meanwhile, Rainbow released 'On Stage', a double live album featuring the now defunct line-up of Blackmore, Dio, Bain, Carey & Powell to fill the gap while formulating the latest version of the band and working on new tracks in France. The album, taken from recordings in Germany and Japan, excellently captures Rainbow at this time and begs the question why Blackmore felt it important to change the line-up once again. Of course it cannot be known for certain what was going on behind the scenes but this line-up, based on the evidence from this album, works on every level. The scene is set with an excerpt from Judy Garland's classic 1939 film 'The Wizard Of Oz', 'we must be over the rainbow'. In case the audience was in any doubt about that statement, Blackmore launches into 'Kill The King', a track that would appear on the next studio album. Just listening to the vinyl album, you can visualise Dio working every inch of the stage and Blackmore taking his stance to the right of Cozy Powell's driving force linking effectively with Jimmy Bain's bass. Tony Carey comes into his own during the blues section in the middle of a medley principally formed of 'Man On A Silver Mountain' and 'Starstruck'. The blues section is a real gem in an otherwise full on album, with Blackmore and Carey's interplay working the lines beautifully before it gives way to the rest of the medley, moving through 'Starstruck' and coming back to 'Silver Mountain' and the return of Dio. Surely his vocals have never been better, and with all due consideration to his later hugely successful career, this album captures him at his very peak of showmanship. He possessed such a powerful voice that he could even dominate above Blackmore's roaring guitar riffs and Powell's strident drumming. To change the scene completely, the band shifts gear into a moving 'Catch The Rainbow' and within the first twenty minutes of this

28

concert have reminded us of their vast depth of range across the whole spectrum of what Rainbow was about. Despite capturing the band before the latest personnel changes and being again rather short for a double album, it satisfied a rock buying public who had become hungry for all things Rainbow. In fairness regarding the disappointment about the length of the album, it should be remembered that live albums were notoriously difficult to fit onto the vinyl format and that many live albums of the era suffered as a result, in particular bands such as Rainbow who were quite capable of launching into extended versions of album tracks and joining whole sections together, making editing a potential nightmare. For example, the superbly intense live version of 'Catch The Rainbow' captured here clocks in at just over fifteen and a half minutes, and 'Mistreated', a track from Blackmore's Purple days, is timed at just over thirteen. So there you have it: one side of vinyl full and ready to rock. In an era of great live albums, this holds its place among the elite and provides a great historical document of the band with Blackmore and Dio combining to give the audience an experience to remember years later. The album moves through 'Sixteenth Century Greensleeves' and a massive 'Still I'm Sad', both taken from the first album, before closing.

Meanwhile the band changes were stuttering. Blackmore had taken Rainbow down to a chateau south of Paris, France initially minus Jimmy Bain and Tony Carey. As stated, Mark Clarke had been brought in to cover bass but only lasted a few weeks before leaving. Clarke had come through the ranks playing with bands like Jon Hiseman's Colosseum, a band that delighted in intricate time changes and a jazz style that only an extremely competent bass player would be able to perform. He later joined Uriah Heep, co-writing, with Ken Hensley, 'The Wizard' on their successful 'Demons & Wizards' album before having to bow out halfway through a tour of the United States, citing health reasons. He was replaced by the late great Gary Thain in Heep and later appeared on some of Ken Hensley's solo albums whilst also working with Ian Hunter and Mountain. Clarke's quick departure from the sessions resulted in Blackmore covering bass whilst he looked for yet another replacement. It wasn't long before Tony Carey left for good to be replaced by ex-Symphonic Slam keyboardist David Stone. Blackmore had heard Stone on the radio and made an approach to him to cover the keys for the forthcoming album.

Despite the uncertainty regarding personnel, the sessions were going well and the band's nucleus of Blackmore, Dio and Cozy Powell were busy writing material that would finally be released as 'Long Live Rock 'n' Roll'. The gap left by the departures of Bain and Clarke finally resulted in Rainbow auditioning Australian bass player Bob Daisley. He joined in May 1977 and is credited with the bass on the subsequent album. Daisley had earned his reputation both with the band Widowmaker and earlier in his career with Chicken Shack, whom he joined on his arrival in London in 1972. He is also credited as pioneering the six-string bass. Widowmaker should and could have been huge but some familiar rock demons would curtail their progress. The band possessed the quality of the likes of lead singer Steve Ellis and guitarist Luther Grosvenor (also known as Ariel Bender), but despite being signed to Don Arden's Jet Records and touring with The Who and The Electric Light Orchestra, they somehow failed to achieve as much as they should have. When Ellis left the band to be replaced by John Butler, they released a second album, 'Too Late To Cry', but by then Widowmaker's time was limited and Daisley left to team up with Mungo Jerry (also known as Jerry Dorsey). Dorsey's band included Dick Middleton, who just happened to know Ritchie Blackmore. As a result of this connection, he was offered the Rainbow slot, and Daisley didn't need too much convincing that this was a great opportunity for him. His post-Rainbow career confirms his status; he went on to play with Uriah Heep, Black Sabbath, guitar virtuoso Yngwie Malmsteen, Gary Moore and Ozzy Osbourne, with whom he was destined to be involved in a court case, along with Uriah Heep drummer Lee Kerslake, over alleged payment problems concerning both Ozzy and his manager Sharon Osbourne, the daughter of Jet Records owner Don Arden. He would also team up once again with Dio. Also, recently he has been part of the Living Loud project along with Don Airey (Rainbow and Deep Purple), Steve Morse (Purple), fellow Australian Jimmy Barnes and Lee Kerslake. Bob Daisley's presence in Rainbow once again lifted the overall quality of the band and the latest line-up, the fourth different version in their relatively short history, listed Blackmore, Dio, Powell and Daisley, and it was to this combination that David Stone was added on keyboards. This line-up was destined to last less than a year when a huge internal disagreement all but split the band.

David Stone had joined from an outfit known as Symphonic Slam, who are best remembered for guitarist Timo Laine's early use of synthesized guitar. He would later go on to play with American rockers Le Mans. During his short stay at Rainbow, he would show that he could certainly cover the keyboards with some impressive offerings.

Rainbow's third studio album 'Long Live Rock 'n' Roll' finally came out in 1978, but not before the new line-up embarked on a major European tour starting in September 1977. A live extended-play single was released by Polydor, and the band arrived in the United Kingdom for sold-out dates throughout that November. However, when they performed a concert in Austria, Ritchie Blackmore found himself held overnight in a local jail cell following an alleged dust-up with a security guard. The set list contained some of the new material and took on an even heavier edge than that of the past. In December 1977 the band stopped touring to complete the album. The cover featured a superb drawing by Debbie Hall, showing each member in a mass of hair; the producer was once again Martin Birch. The Bavarian String Ensemble were utilised on both 'Gates Of Babylon' and 'Rainbow Eyes'. Once again, all tracks are credited to the writing team of Blackmore and Dio with Cozy Powell chipping in on 'The Shed'. This, sadly, was to be the last Rainbow album featuring Ronnie James Dio and therefore is worthy of a close and critical look.

The album's opener 'Long Live Rock n Roll' is a surefire winner, kicking in with a fire burst from drummer Cozy, and was guaranteed to achieve years of airplay as it was released as a single. Commercial? Undoubtedly, but whilst more than a little repetitive, it also showcases the Dio and Blackmore combination, a pairing that was about to implode just as it put Rainbow well and truly into the mainstream. Despite the straight-ahead commercialism of the opener, the album has an altogether heavier feel, and the second track, 'Lady Of The Lake', reflects the darker mood of much of the material that followed. It is atmospheric and haunting with typically Dio imagination in the lyrics. 'L.A. Connection' features an instantly recognisable Blackmore riff and is a powerhouse of a song with great vocals from Dio, surely one of the best rock vocalists ever. The well-produced track is positioned perfectly on the album and provides the ideal lead into the classic Dio vision of 'Gates Of Babylon'. Intensely eerie and driven along within a wonderfully evocative Arabian atmosphere, it contains all of Dio's power of imagination in its lyrical fantasy journey. Despite it being a drummer's nightmare with constant time changes, Cozy Powell, of course, pulls it off superbly with just the right feel as the track moves through varying emotional senses whilst telling a disturbing story full of mystery and darkness. It comes straight from the rich vein of material from which 'Stargazer' had previously emerged, but sadly the Dio / Blackmore partnership was running down and this would be the last such epic. 'Kill The King' is an all-out assault that became a part of Rainbow's live set, featuring amazing and near impossible dexterity by Blackmore. 'Shed (subtle)' comes next and once again hits the mark. Rainbow had somehow managed to follow the excellent 'Rising' album with a killer fantasy metal album containing medieval darkness in abundance and musicianship that is of the highest possible quality. Despite the almost constant change within the band's line-up, Blackmore was still able, at this stage, to tie the band together to produce one of the major rock albums of the era. To follow 'Rising' with an album as dramatic as this was near impossible, but they somehow remained focussed enough to deliver. Unfortunately, it was to be the last that included Dio. If the next track, 'Sensitive To Light' seems a little predictable, then that statement alone speaks literal volumes for the rest of the material on offer. Rainbow had achieved all this and consequently left us with a rich memory of what this band could produce. Back-to-back albums such as 'Rising' and 'Long Live Rock n Roll' are rare indeed. The album ends with the sadly sensitive 'Rainbow Eyes', Dio's last track with the band, sung with surprising subtlety. It rounds off a set as good as anything that Rainbow would ever produce.

Quite why this line-up split so totally after this album is a mystery that only the players involved could ever really answer, but maybe it would have been asking too much, even of this pairing, to continue to produce this quality of music. Either way Ritchie Blackmore has never been one to follow a conventional path, and therein lies the genius of the man. He quite simply would not rest on his achievements but seemingly felt the need to constantly push himself further in different directions and along different roads by reinventing not only himself but his band. It is impossible to say what Rainbow with Dio on board would have gone on to produce. He was, after all, the writer of the lyrics that so perfectly captured Blackmore's desire to produce music planted firmly within a medieval or historical setting and his loss diminished the effect to an alarming extent. The band continued to evolve and morph with further changes of personnel and, post-Rainbow, Dio would go on to claim the heavy metal vocal crown that he so thoroughly deserves. Blackmore, ultimately, would reinvent himself for perhaps the last time to write and perform full on Renaissance music with Blackmore's Night. This was the last in a trio of albums by Rainbow that achieved what the band had originally set out to do. That was to produce music with more than a passing nod towards long departed classical composers such as Bach and echo an historical style of music that had long since been lost to the world in general through the medium of rock. It was an interesting challenge, but one that on the evidence of the first three albums they achieved to an extraordinarily high level.

Unfortunately, the clouds were once again gathering and by August 1978, the band all but self-destructed. Not only did Ronnie James Dio leave, apparently following a major dispute with Blackmore, but he was quickly followed out the door by both Bob Daisley and David Stone. This left just Blackmore and Powell as yet more replacements were sought. Dio's subsequent career confirms his high standing amongst the rock elite. Consistently voted among the best front men in the history of the genre, he went from strength to strength in such bands as Black Sabbath and his own Dio. There was a huge sense of dismay when Dio announced that he had left Rainbow, but this was somehow tempered by the sense of the inevitable. Ritchie Blackmore had gained a reputation for being almost impossible to work with, but he saw Rainbow as very much his own band and strongly believed that he could take them in whatever direction he chose. Despite being sacked after only a year of impressive performances on bass, Bob Daisley speaks highly of Blackmore. In an interview on the Cosmik Debris website, dated August 2002, when questioned about some of the strongly negative views about and names given to the guitarist by other musicians he says, 'A lot of people think that. I've never termed Ritchie a 'jerk'. I think he is a really, really dedicated musician and it was good, the discipline and the tenacity of him it helped run things like a well oiled engine'. Whatever the view is on Blackmore and whatever it is that was driving him at this stage in his career, you cannot argue about his achievements. There does, however, seem to be a recurring part of his character that likes to challenge and confront not only the situation he has created or finds himself in but also himself, and it seems that once he feels too comfortable in any given situation, he literally takes it down and starts again. The exception is Blackmore's Night, and whether that is something to do with maturity or whether he is genuinely happy and content to finally be allowed to produce the music that really interests him is only something he or the people closest to him can answer. Rainbow was his band, his creation and totally under his control. The fact of the matter was that in August 1978, the band split in two, and once again he found himself trying to create a new setup. This time it would be even harder because he had lost the voice of the band in Dio. Perhaps that was the exact type of situation he thrived upon, representing another major challenge in an all-too-unpredictable career; only time would tell if he could once again conjure up such magical combinations that had taken Rainbow to the very top.

34

CHAPTER FOUR

Replacing a vocalist and front man of the calibre of Ronnie James Dio was never going to be easy. Whilst searching for the answer, Blackmore made the surprising move to recruit former Deep Purple colleague, bass player Roger Glover. Glover had been busy making a name for himself as a writer and producer, and it was those skills as much as his undoubted ability as a bass player that attracted Blackmore to approach him. Glover also had the reputation for producing some commercial return for bands, and his inclusion was a sign that Rainbow wanted to follow up the previous success of the title track from 'Long Live Rock n Roll' with more commercial releases. Glover had been close to forming a band with Dio at the time that Blackmore had invited Elf along to form Rainbow and since that time had been working on several solo projects including the album 'Elements', which featured ex-Elf and Rainbow keyboard player Mickey Lee Soule.

On joining Rainbow, Glover was reunited with Ritchie Blackmore for the first time since their days in Deep Purple and set about writing material for the forthcoming Rainbow follow up to 'Long Live Rock n Roll'.

Blackmore meanwhile recruited Don Airey on keyboards. Airey, destined to fill Jon Lord's seat in Deep Purple, had already enjoyed a successful career and, classically trained, was ideal for Blackmore's continued vision for Rainbow. He had already played with Cozy Powell in Hammer and had also teamed up briefly with Black Sabbath, appearing on their album 'Never Say Die'. Don Airey was later to play with the likes of Ozzy Osbourne, producing the wonderful introduction to the track 'Mr Crowley' on 'Blizzard of Oz' and several other albums, toured with Jethro Tull in the late eighties, worked with Maiden's Bruce Dickinson, helped out Gary Moore, recorded a solo album 'K2' and is now with Deep Purple. Airey and Glover's recruitment coincided with the arrival of the band's new voice, Graham Bonnet. Englishman Bonnet had appeared in several bands, namely Bluesect, Bonar Law and The Graham Bonnet Set before meeting Robert Stigwood and forming a duo with his cousin Trevor Gordon called The Marbles. The Marbles enjoyed a brief period of success, notably the 1968 single 'Only One Woman', produced by The Bee Gees, and a self-titled album. When the duo fell apart in 1969, Bonnet joined Southern Comfort as a bass player before releasing three solo singles between 1972-1974: 'Whisper In The Night', 'Trying To Say Goodbye' and 'Back Row In The Stalls', all to limited success. In 1974 he appeared in a film called 'Three For All' as a singer in a rock group. Three years later he released a solo album called simply 'Graham Bonnet' and a single 'It's All Over Now Baby Blue' and followed this with a second solo album called 'No Bad Habit'. When Ritchie Blackmore contacted him and asked him to join, he put his solo career on hold and was soon fronting Rainbow. Once again his tenure within Rainbow would be relatively short-lived, but in that time he sang on some of the band's most commercially successful chart songs including 'Since You Been Gone'. After Rainbow he released a third solo album before meeting up with Cozy Powell again in The Michael Schenker Group. In 1983 he formed his own band Alcatrazz, who enjoyed a solid following and released three albums. When Alcatrazz came to an end in 1987, he had spells in the bands Impellitteri and Forcefield, and released a further three solo albums, 1991's 'Here Comes The Night', 1996's 'Underground' and lastly 'The Day I Went Mad' in 1999. At the time he joined Rainbow, however, he was seen as a surprise choice. He had a bluesier voice than that of Dio and he therefore fitted well into Blackmore's proposed minor switch of gears for Rainbow.

This new line-up of Blackmore, Powell, Glover, Airey and Bonnet, Rainbow's fifth, began work together in March 1979. Most of the album that would become 'Down To Earth' was already in shape, and on Bonnet's arrival the vocal tracks were laid down and the album quickly completed. The band took on a more commercial stance, and the two monster hits from the album, 'All Night Long' and 'Since You Been Gone', seemingly justified Blackmore's judgement. In retrospect this album is neither one style nor another and represents a period of transition in the band's history. Bonnet covered the vocals to good effect, adding his own blues grit to the sound, and Roger Glover, who had taken over production from Martin Birch, fulfilled his aim through the resulting chart successes. The album cover is a rather typical late seventies effort by Ron Walotsky, showing Earth from space linked in orbit by the trademark rainbow. Opening with the hit 'All Night Long', a track written by the restored partnership of Blackmore and Glover, the album was a watered-down version of Rainbow's previous work but with its more commercial feel was destined for chart success. Gone are the fantasy lyrics of Dio and gone too was his huge presence. This is not to say that Graham Bonnet was not up to the role; his performances are remembered by the mainstream as being perhaps more representative of Rainbow's music at that time, due to the almost continuous radio exposure the band was enjoying. His was a rasping blues voice that hit the mark in this era for the band. The second track 'Eyes Of The World' continues in the same vein, and Bonnet rises to the cause with some vocal acrobatics that helped secure his acceptance by the Rainbow faithful. The album is very much an album of its time and therefore did not push any boundaries as the previous three had succeeded in doing. 'No Time To Lose' sounds like another formatted song but one that suits Bonnet's style well. On first play, back in 1979, I can remember waiting for a killer epic Rainbow track, a 'Stargazer' or a 'Gates Of Babylon' perhaps, and feeling rather desolate as the album trundled along without one. Those days had gone; Rainbow had shifted direction and come up with an album that on one level rocks and on another provides two of Rainbows best-known moments but still somehow frustrates and disappoints. The old side one ends with 'Makin' Love' which starts promisingly with some Rainbowesque sequences but once again just doesn't reach the heights. It is strange that this album provided Rainbow with its peak of commercial sales, particularly with 'Since You Been Gone', while to many Rainbow fans it actually represented the beginning of a decline, an album aimed at a broader audience and in the process lost something of the mystery of previous Rainbow albums.

It is all but impossible to turn this album over and play track one, side two without being influenced by the fact that this track is one of the most played radio tracks of all time: 'Since You Been Gone'. Quite literally we have all heard this track countless times; it is played as often today on any classic rock station as any other track by any other band. Let's face it: it is the perfect radio track, just slightly over the standard three minutes.

Photo: Pictorial Press

It does, however, have that killer Blackmore riff once again proving what a master of his art he can be and that exquisitely effective guitar break that had you playing it over and over again. So as tempting as it is to hark back to the dungeons, demons and castles fantasy of Dio, who can argue when a heavily restructured band comes out with a monster single like this? In the same vein, it would have been impossible in Dio's absence for Rainbow to continue along the same path, and by taking this turn and performing material of this strength, Blackmore had once again turned adversity into success. The track was actually written by Russ Ballard, once of Argent, and shifts gear continuously with some ear-catching sequences that keep the interest during what could have been an annoyingly repetitive song. In fact, the original Ballard version is now impossible to listen to in light of how huge the Rainbow interpretation became. Ballard's track record is beyond doubt; he is also responsible for 'God Gave Rock n Roll To You', a massive hit for Argent that was later covered by Kiss, 'So You Win Again' made a hit by Hot Chocolate, and scored another huge hit with 'You Can Do Magic'. 'Since You Been Gone' is almost formula chart rock, but the magic of Blackmore's guitar transforms it into one of the most instantly recognisable tracks of all time. Back to back with Boston's 'More Than A Feeling', these two tracks could epitomise everything that is considered classic mainstream rock. Blackmore's belief in the new direction of Rainbow was somewhat vindicated by its success. Surprisingly, 'All Night Long' reached number five in the UK charts while the better-known 'Since You Been Gone' peaked at six. The album itself hit the same position.

'Love's No Friend' returns us to the Blackmore/Glover material and is a good showcase for Graham Bonnet's blues-based vocals. It is little surprise that this was to be his only album with the band and despite the massive success, he joined the now huge cast of ex-Rainbow members only a year later. 'Danger Zone' and 'Lost in Hollywood' bring this album to a close. As a whole, it tends to divide opinion like no other Rainbow album and is very much a step taken away from what was expected towards something altogether rewarding, albeit in a different way. There is a brief and tantalising return to a Moroccan theme in 'Danger Zone' and Bonnet's vocals are effective and confident, but he really opens out as the album rocks to the conclusion of 'Lost In Hollywood'. Ironically, this would be Bonnet's last recorded track with the band before packing his vocals and heading out of Rainbow, destined to be forever remembered as the singer on some of their biggest-ever hits that continue to be heard on radios all over the world. He did, however, appear with the band when they headlined the Monsters Of Rock Festival in August 1980. Once again stability and Rainbow did not go hand in hand, and the festival also proved to be Cozy Powell's swan song with the band as he left to join The Michael Schenker Group. Blackmore responded by hiring American drummer Bobby Rondinelli to fill the massive gap left by Powell, who stated that the lurch towards a more commercial and poppy sound had caused him to leave.

Drummer Bobby Rondinelli originated from Port Jefferson in New York State, where he had played with The Wanderers. He joined Rainbow and quickly went to work on the sessions that would become the 1981 album 'Difficult To Cure'. His stint with Rainbow was to last until they were disbanded in 1984 and helped establish his reputation to such an extent that he went on to play with Blue Oyster Cult, Black Sabbath and The Lizards.

Following Graham Bonnet's departure, Blackmore once again began to look for a new vocalist and quickly drafted another American, Joe Lynn Turner, previously of Ezra and the AOR band Fandango, who had released several albums but had recently disbanded. Turner was also very familiar with a lot of early Deep Purple material, as he had covered them quite extensively in his earlier career. So when Blackmore came calling and with the knowledge that the band also included another much admired ex-Purple member, Roger Glover, Joe jumped at the chance. Not only was Turner a good choice possessing a strong voice, but he also looked good and wrote solid AOR material that would help Rainbow finally establish themselves in the States. Always huge in Europe, particularly Germany, Japan and the United Kingdom, it wasn't until MTV picked up on the big-selling singles and accompanying videos that Rainbow really cracked America. With an American front man in Turner, Rainbow was suddenly bigger news across the Atlantic. As a writer he was co-credited with a couple of tracks on his first Rainbow album. It was a modest start, but by the time of his second Rainbow album, 'Straight Between The Eyes', he had really found his feet and was credited with co-writing all nine tracks. Joe Lynn Turner had a stage presence that fitted what Rainbow was trying to achieve at that time, and his tenure at the front proved a popular one as the band went from strength to strength. He could belt out the best-known tracks as competently as any other, and even though his voice wasn't as strong as Ronnie James Dio, he made up for it with the right stage image and versatility. In an era when the video came of age and appearance began to take on a more important role, he had it all—so much that it became all but impossible to watch MTV without seeing one of the band's songs. It was a format that fellow ex-Purple singer David Coverdale would work so effectively with his own band Whitesnake. The two bands are intrinsically linked and the family tree of Rainbow, Deep Purple and Whitesnake is a complicated one. The crossover of talent among the three UK bands provided a never-ending merry-go-round of line-up changes. Therefore, it wasn't just Rainbow who would confound with change upon change; the same can be said of Whitesnake, Deep Purple and the huge ever-changing situation that always seemed to be a feature of Black Sabbath. In 1983 Sabbath stunned just about everyone by recruiting Ian Gillan to front them. It was a combination that spawned one dubious release, the album 'Born Again'. Such was the fluidity of movement at the time. Rainbow's own family tree contained a rich array of talent over the years and included some of the best exponents of their craft available at that particular time. This latest Rainbow combination of Blackmore, Turner and Glover proved a successful one. Not only did they all remain in Rainbow until its suspension but also all appeared in Deep Purple Mark 5 between 1989 and 1992, appearing on the album 'Slaves And Masters' before Turner was replaced by the returning Ian Gillan. The Rainbow-Purple connection went a step further when Turner collaborated with ex-Purple bass player Glenn Hughes in the Hughes Turner project. He has also worked with guitarist Yngwie Malmsteen.

By November 1980 the latest line-up of Blackmore, Glover, Airey, Turner and Rondinelli, or Rainbow Six, completed the album 'Difficult To Cure' and it was subsequently released early in the next year. It is best remembered for containing, in fact opening with, Rainbow's biggest-ever hit single, 'I Surrender', another Russ Ballard-penned monster. Produced once again by Roger Glover, it had been recorded in Copenhagen. Unfortunately, it is also remembered for one of the worst covers in an era full of equally bad examples. In a design by Hipgnosis, seven masked surgeons peer at you from behind surgical masks on the front cover whilst on the back of the album they return with the welcome addition of an attractive nurse looking down at you on the operating table. It is a truly awful cover, further underlined by a disturbing array of surgical instruments laid out on the inner sleeve.

Once again, Rainbow fans were left not really knowing what to expect, but the album opens strongly with the played-to-death UK chart success 'I Surrender', a song that took Rainbow to their highest position ever at number three. As commercial as this song, along with the previous singles, undoubtedly was, the songs worked very well in a live situation as they still contained strong power chords and examples of Blackmore at his best, enabling Rainbow to deliver full-on and powerful live versions. Having said that, this song in particular is the definition of commercialised pop itself and is a clear indication of where the band wanted to be at that time. Record sales speak volumes of course, and the song's success cannot be argued against, but all things considered it was tracks like this that had the original Rainbow fans wondering just what was coming next. By opening the album with this track it followed on neatly from 'Down To Earth', but whether this was a particularly good point is open to debate. Ritchie Blackmore had moved the band into the centre ground and the shift had resulted in worldwide success and recognition, but when hearing this track for the first time opening this album you cannot help but feel that along the way he had lost some of the original aims of the band including his love and inclusion of classical and Renaissance themes. This is out-and-out pop but delivered so professionally that the song is lifted above the norm with some solid power performances. Anyone who had concerns over the arrival of a third vocalist in as many years would have been impressed with Joe Lynn Turner's start. All things said, Dio was an impossible act to follow, but the band had moved direction and with material such as this being the aim, Turner was the right choice and voice whilst also looking the part.

Needless to say, these hits became firm fixtures in the set lists with the fans loving every minute. Where the band had lost out during this phase is on songwriting. Long gone were Dio's mystical lyrics resulting in adventures put to epic tracks. Now the band was very much into writing the three- or four-minute track. The most successful singles had been written outside the band and there is an apparent lack of depth on this album that hadn't been felt before. The second track 'Spotlight Kid' gives Don Airey a chance to showcase his undoubted skills on keyboards, ability that would one day result in him occupying the legendary Jon Lord's position in Deep Purple. It is a standard rocker saved from itself by the Airey section and Turner's confident vocals. It is a different sound and style from the Dio years but when played loud, allowing Blackmore's guitar to really hit home, makes you realise how powerful their music continued to be. 'No Release' arrives with a Blackmore opening, trademark killer riffs and a co-credit to Don Airey along with the now established songwriting team of Blackmore and Glover. Once again the track opens into a Blackmore solo that acts as a strong reminder of what this band can do and what a guitarist he is. This is the closest in feel and atmosphere to the Rainbow of old and once again needs volume to really bring it to life. The Blackmore solo is another example of what ignites this band and lifts it to an altogether higher level. This far into the album it is apparent that this latest incarnation of Rainbow is meshing together well, and whether or not the material is perceived as better or perhaps worse, than that offered in the past, the musicianship is of the usual highest standards. Bobby Rondinelli is a powerful, driving drummer and machine-guns his way through tracks, particularly when playing live. Don Airey is given room to perform on keys to excellent effect. Roger Glover's bass is as competent and relevant as ever, and as discussed Joe Lynn Turner knew exactly how to perform songs like 'I Surrender'. All things having been taken into consideration, particularly what the band was about at this time, it worked.

Unfortunately, then comes the track 'Magic'. I found it hard on first play of this album to even begin to reconcile why one of the world's most gifted guitarists would want to put his name to this type of song. It is poppy, trashy, repetitive and absolutely nothing to do with what we were used to from Rainbow. It could have and in the ideal world should have been covered by someone else. Obviously, it was destined for single release

and duly came out after 'I Surrender' and its follow-up 'Can't Happen Here'. It sold well but the end result is that, on hearing this, to admit to liking Rainbow after it had been all over the radio was tantamount to advertising that you liked this kind of chart song, and I'm afraid I just couldn't do that. The situation is perhaps best looked at by putting my own personal opinions to one side and trawling the internet to see what other Rainbow fans were thinking at the time. Once again, you cannot argue with commercial success in terms of money or raising a profile by gaining airplay and subsequently selling out arenas, but it is obviously a track that divides feelings into two quite separate camps. You cannot sit on the fence with this. You either like it and support what the band was trying to achieve or you hate it and mourn the fact that rock masters like Blackmore, Airey and Glover could even consider putting their collective names to it. Fortunately, they didn't write it, and I am not necessarily knocking the song as a pop record as it is a well-constructed, catchy piece for that arena, but I am questioning whether a band like Rainbow was right to take it on. It is somewhat redeemed by the opening gunfire drumming by Rondinelli and Blackmore's almost throwaway sequence and typically smooth solo. Turner sings it well and the lyrics are good, but what a band like Rainbow was thinking of going down this road is beyond me. On various websites I can see that many people will disagree, and of course it was destined to be a song that divided opinions strongly. Quite what Dio or Cozy Powell would have made of it is open to conjecture, but you can almost sense their horror. Side one is somewhat rescued by the Blackmore/Airey instrumental 'Vielleicht Das Nächster Mal' – incorrectly translated as 'Maybe Next Time' on the aforementioned terrible album cover. It's melodic, smooth and thankfully returns to some of Blackmore's original ideas and themes for the whole Rainbow project. It is a beautifully constructed track that once again caused disagreement among the ranks, being as hard for the new fans who had arrived via the singles' successes to comprehend as it was for the likes of me, dating back fondly to Stargazer, to accept its predecessor. It goes without saying that Blackmore gives another virtuoso performance. Rarely have I heard such a clean and precise guitarist as this man, a statement that seemingly contradicts his intense personality. It is this constant searching and reinvention that left us in no doubt that he continually strived for perfection and was constantly looking for the future.

This phrase brings us neatly to the opener on side two, 'Can't Happen Here'. Written by the Blackmore and Glover combination, the lyrics are clever and interesting and as a result, it actually sounds like a Rainbow song whilst giving Joe Lyn Turner a great chance to show just what he can do; it's an opportunity that he doesn't let pass him by. It proved to be a marginally successful single. The singer appears among the credits for the next track 'Freedom Fighter', another well-worked song whose end result is not exceptional. It moves along quickly and gives way to 'Midtown Tunnel Vision' a song that kicks off with a nod to Hendrix during the opening sequence before slinking along like a slowly burning fuse before Blackmore sets it alight with yet another stunning solo. A strong track and an album highlight, it works superbly well and picks up side two effectively, leading into the album's title track 'Difficult To Cure'. Suddenly and surprisingly and with a slight sense of relief, after all that has gone before, we are transported back to Ritchie Blackmore's classical influences. It is a reminder of what made Rainbow different in the first place and shoots a huge hole in the theory of a relentless move towards commercialism. Not only is it a showcase for Blackmore but the whole band with Rondinelli slavishly working through a mammoth amount of time changes and Don Airey putting his own classical training to good effect as well with a rousing organ solo. The whole thing is of course based on Beethoven's magnificent Ninth Symphony (Opus 125 in D Minor – often referred to as 'Choral' or 'Ode To Joy') written nearly 160 years earlier. It brings to an end a totally confusing album – confusingly – and when the fairground laughter akin to the laughing policeman chillingly sounds out the record you cannot help but wonder what Blackmore is trying to say. Was the joke on us?

The reviews were very mixed, to say the least. For once Rainbow had released an album seemingly without their trademark co-ordination. Previous to this, their albums had been well thought out and balanced, where tracks led naturally into the next and thereby created a whole rather than a disjointed and confusing record that sent out a whole range of messages. The album contained the singles 'I Surrender', 'Can't Happen Here' and the previously discussed 'Magic' but also included the musical interlude of 'Vielleicht Das Nächster Mal' and 'Difficult To Cure'. They didn't sit well together, and fans of the band were left somewhat puzzled over where Rainbow was going and which Rainbow would appear next. On the one hand, every time you turned on the radio 'Since You Been Gone' or 'All Night Long' sounded out, and on the other, the band delved into Blackmore's classical ideas once more. Was it just as important to Blackmore to resolutely hang on to those critical early influences whilst simultaneously opting for a more mainstream sound? For people buying the album on the strength of the singles it must have been confusing, but for people dating back to Dio and the 'Rising' period, the mixed messages caused mental mayhem. Where would Ritchie Blackmore take this band next?

First he took them on a tour of America, where for the first time they headlined, a fact that in itself seemingly justified the commercial shift that Rainbow had undertaken. Meanwhile, the album was busy rising to number three in the UK charts. The single 'Kill The King' was re-released as was the first album 'Ritchie

Blackmore's Rainbow' which of course featured an entirely different line-up. A further band change occurred after the subsequent World Tour when in August 1981 Don Airey quit and left for fresh challenges, to be replaced by another classically trained keyboard player, American David Rosenthal. After graduating from Boston's highly regarded Berklee College Of Music with an incredible triple major in Piano Performance, Electronic Music and Audio, he played with Morning Thunder, Crystal Visions and a band called Masterpiece. Blackmore could clearly see that he was not only getting a talented keyboard player, but also someone with an amazing array of technical skills. His subsequent career confirms this and he has worked extensively with Billy Joel, toured with Elton John and Bruce Springsteen, appeared with Whitesnake, Stevie Vai and Yngwie Malmsteen and has also written Broadway shows such as the award winning 'Moving Out', for which he not only wrote the keyboard parts but was also responsible for programming and producing the classical playback tracks. He has subsequently worked in the classical field with both The Czech Philharmonic and The New Japan Philharmonic Orchestra. Returning full circle, he lectures at The Berklee, who have recently awarded him their 'Distinguished Alumni Award for Outstanding Achievements in Contemporary Music.' Clearly a highly respected musician sharing similar classical inspirations as Blackmore, he found himself in Rainbow and quickly at work on the band's next studio album. Meanwhile, 'The Best Of Rainbow' album was released in 1981 containing such typically diverse offerings as 'Stargazer', 'Sixteenth Century Greensleeves', 'All Night Long' and 'I Surrender'. It moved rather disjointedly from one line-up to another and back and didn't seem to follow any logical sense of progress. It ended with the Rainbow version of 'Mistreated'.

Rainbow Mark Seven, now consisting of Blackmore, Glover, Turner, Rondinelli and Rosenthal, were destined to become the longest surviving line-up. The band now consisted of three Americans, Turner, Rondinelli and Rosenthal, and that along with the fact that Roger Glover was also living in Connecticut at the time possibly influenced the decision to record outside of Europe for the first time in the band's history: they eventually chose Canada and moved into Le Studio in Morin Heights.

The sessions, which were to result in Rainbow's sixth studio album 'Straight Between The Eyes', took place very early in 1982 with the album finally being released that April. In truth the album, albeit a more co-ordinated effort than 'Difficult To Cure', continued along the path towards AOR and by this time the band had lost many of the original fan base. That said, it can be seen as a return to form with some more characteristic and welcome heavier sounds. The album cover, again by Hipgnosis, doesn't improve much on the previous effort: it depicts Ritchie's Fender arm smashing through the forehead of someone with a rainbow in their eye.

The band's name is printed in huge letters across the top and on the back, each of the band member's eyes stare out at you. Inside there is a studio portrait photograph of the band showing a tired-looking Ritchie Blackmore, a young-looking David Rosenthal and the incredible, large hair of Bobby Rondinelli.

As if stung by some of the criticism in the reviews of 'Difficult To Cure' the new writing partnership of Blackmore and Turner open the album with 'Death Alley Driver', a return to a more solid, heavy rock sound that is very much appreciated and injects some welcome energy back into the band. It could be that it took this time for the various writing combinations to finally gel, but either way this is an opener that really kick-starts the album. Blackmore launches into an incredibly fast solo with teasing classical undertones before stepping back and giving new keyboard man David Rosenthal the space to show exactly what he could do with the same theme. Leaving you somewhat breathless, the band bring you back down with the next track, a beautifully executed ballad that was released as a single. 'Stone Cold' must rank as one of Joe Lynn Turner's finest Rainbow moments. He sings with huge doses of sensitivity and tenderness and delivers the song, which he co-wrote with Blackmore and Glover, perfectly. It is a real emotion tugger and helps to highlight the fact that JLT was exactly the right man in exactly the right place performing exactly the right type of music during this particular phase of the Rainbow story.

'Bring On The Night (Dream Chaser)' is track three and opens interestingly enough before becoming somewhat predictable despite the colour of Blackmore's solo lifting it up temporarily. This track really highlights how the songwriting team of Blackmore, Glover and Turner were aiming in part at least for a radio-friendly sound but by so doing it cannot be overlooked that the band was losing something along the way. Rainbow had always been strong on originality, producing atmospheric and unique soundscapes, and had previously been true to the band's influences and strengths by producing well-constructed and meaningful rock, but with this sort of track, particularly as it is written by two ex-Deep Purple members and one future one, it all becomes harder to enjoy. It is almost throwaway and lightweight eighties rock and could have been by any one of a number of bands occupying the same AOR slot at that time. It does not have that Rainbow stamp on it and I am confused as to why the likes of Blackmore and Glover would be satisfied producing such average songs. I am tempted to suggest that once Blackmore had travelled this far along on the commercial bandwagon, conquered stadiums, achieved chart success and more MTV coverage than he could have hoped or dreamed of, he quickly grew tired of and frustrated by what he had created and subsequently stepped out in another act of re-invention and rejoined Deep Purple. The track's saving graces are that it is well produced,

has great sound and for the market it is aimed at is well-written and performed; still, it has very little substance and as already stated it could have been done just as well by any one of a number of bands. Somehow Rainbow had moved away from their independent and therefore interesting influences. A character as mystically inspired and uniquely gifted as Blackmore had seemingly sold the family jewels for some airplay, and this realisation through tracks such as 'Magic' from the 'Difficult To Cure' album and 'Bring On the Night' from this, the latest offering, confused, confounded and annoyed many Rainbow followers. Of course the loss of a percentage of Rainbow fans would be more than compensated by the attraction of more, albeit from a different fan base. Blackmore, never one to operate within boundaries, was now taking the band into a completely different area.

That said, 'Straight Between The Eyes' is a far more balanced and cohesive album than 'Difficult To Cure'. This statement suggests that the band had finally abandoned most of the glimpses of the past that had appeared on 'Difficult To Cure' to the confusion of the overall effort for a slicker, balanced and more consistently mainstream effort with 'Straight Between The Eyes'. I think it is important in the case of this album, more than any other Rainbow release, to take the album as a whole rather than as individual tracks. Viewed individually there are some disappointments, but taken together the album meshes together quite magically. It is hard, it is superbly produced and it is lifted by some memorable and outstanding moments. The result is a far easier album to listen to than 'Difficult To Cure' because each track fits well together, but it can also be said that it represented a further leap along the path that would ultimately bring the band to an end with Blackmore's return to the battleground that Deep Purple would once again be. The album had opened strongly enough with more than a hint of Deep Purple in 'Death Alley Driver' and then a classic in 'Stone Cold', but here we were stuck midway through in the middle ground once again with 'Bring On The Night (Dream Chaser)'. The fact that, if I do take it in isolation, it doesn't excite or inspire me of course should not overlook the fact that there were many new and older fans alike who lapped it up. Certainly the line-up was perfectly suited to it, and in a live environment Rainbow always maintained its power and drama.

'Tite Squeeze', written by the now familiar trio, is very much along the same lines but leads fittingly into one of the album highlights, 'Tearin' My Heart Out'. Once again Joe Lynn Turner is quite superb in much the same vein as the earlier 'Stone Cold'. Backed atmospherically by Rosenthal's keyboards, the track provides a high point in the album. The album moves on into 'Power', a track that despite its power chords unusually has Blackmore taking an easier, straightforward line. Despite screaming out for airplay and possessing a heavier, driving edge, it is all a little predictable, and even Blackmore struggles to find an angle to inject some of his trademark fireworks into it. This from another band would possibly be reviewed more favourably, but this was Ritchie Blackmore's Rainbow and because of that alone it feels disappointing and unrepresentative of such an array of talent. Taken as part of a set, it opens a strong side of the album that moves through several highs before ending with a wonderful Rainbow gem. 'Miss Mistreated' follows neatly in the same groove and soon became a Rainbow live favourite. It featured the new addition of David Rosenthal's writing skills and increases the overall effect that this is an album that works so much better than its predecessor. 'Miss Mistreated', not to be confused with the Deep Purple track from the 'Burn' days, once again fits perfectly within this side of the album. 'Rock Fever' is an attention-grabber that is driven effectively by the pounding drums of Rondinelli. It contains a spectacular Blackmore solo that reaffirms that the band still possessed his genius, and Joe Lynn Turner's powerful vocals help erase memories of vocalists past. Roger Glover and Bobby Rondinelli are tightly knitted, driving the band forward to produce a superb Rainbow track, but nothing can prepare you for what was to come next. It is 'Eyes Of Fire', credited to Blackmore, Turner and Rondinelli, every bit the exquisite Rainbow track that we all knew they were capable of. It is lush, hauntingly full of mystical Arabic scent and finishes the album on a high. It has production that captures perfectly the whole image of the song and it is just that, a vibrant visual scene rather than just sound. It is another Rainbow treasure and ends the album, making it all but impossible not to turn it over, or in these days press replay, to start the whole journey again. Having gone through the kick-off opener, 'Death Alley Driver', through two moving ballads, 'Stone Cold' and 'Tearin' Out My Heart' and the co-ordinated rock of the second side, we end up here in a Moroccan bazaar with the band pulling out all the stops.

Time never stood still with Rainbow, and every album represents a movement in one way or another. Maybe only now can the reasons behind the constant changes of personnel and shifts in direction be really understood. At the time the changes were dismissed as possibly being an example of its leader being all but impossible to work with or at least difficult to please, but maybe it was just that Blackmore could take the band in any direction that he chose and had the talent to do it successfully, and he did exactly that. In a career that has seen him influence a large part of one of the heaviest albums of its era, Deep Purple's 'In Rock', an album staggeringly ahead of its time and then creating his own classical and Renaissance platform with the early Rainbow through to his full medieval metamorphosis now with Blackmore's Night, it is hardly surprising that he could also spend a while occupying the middle ground to such good effect with some commercial eighties rock.

CHAPTER FIVE

Rainbow took to the road to promote 'Straight Between The Eyes' with a world tour. Whilst the album was moving up to its highest position of five in the UK album charts, the UK was, ironically, the one place that Rainbow didn't perform. Once again a further shock soon came when Bobby Rondinelli was asked to leave the band and fellow American Chuck Burgi was drafted in. Uncertainty over a classic line-up revival of Deep Purple occupied the minds of the rock media, but even though the rumours ultimately proved correct, the actual event was a little way off yet. There was still a little more from Rainbow to come in the eighth line-up of Blackmore, Glover, Turner, Rosenthal and the new drummer Burgi. In truth the sands were rapidly disappearing for Rainbow, and Burgi was destined to occupy the drum stool for only nine months until the band was finally shelved in March 1984. In the meantime, Rainbow went to Denmark to start work on their seventh studio album.

53

57

58

Photo: Pictorial Press

60

61

63

Photo: Pictorial Press

It finally came out in August 1983 and was known as 'Bent Out Of Shape'. It would be their last studio album for over 10 years. Chuck Burgi had been busy working with Blackmore's old Deep Purple colleague Ian Gillan when the call came. Once again Rainbow was three-fifths American, Burgi having been born in New Jersey in 1952. His younger brother is the well-known television, stage and film actor Richard Burgi. According to a link from David Rosenthal's website, Chuck is clearly a natural drummer, having mastered one of his father's favourites, 'Drum Boogie Woogie', at a ridiculously early age. His early influences included Ringo Starr and Mitch Mitchell of The Jimi Hendrix Experience fame. His early career included work with Brand X and Daryl Hall and John Oates, with whom he appeared on two platinum-selling albums. He then moved to a group called Balance and performed session work with the likes of Michael Bolton, Diana Ross and Jon Bon Jovi. His stay at Rainbow was shortened by Ritchie Blackmore's decision to put the band on hold, but during that time he did complete two world tours. After Rainbow he worked again with Joe Lynn Turner on JLT's solo album and teamed up again with Roger Glover. Other noteworthy credits include working with Pat Benatar and forming his own band Skull. He also worked with Meatloaf, going on five world tours with him, and then went to Blue Öyster Cult. At this point he worked alongside another ex-Rainbow colleague, keyboard player David Rosenthal, for a highly regarded album 'Red Dawn'. Work with Enrique Iglasias and Billy Joel followed.

'Bent Out Of Shape' is a fitting finale for this line-up of Rainbow. It is a particular high point for Joe Lynn Turner, whose improvement since 'Difficult To Cure' is well-illustrated here. The album kicks off with 'Stranded', which is a no-nonsense but unspectacular opener. Then comes the organ introduction to 'Can't Let You Go', which leads to another solid performance by Turner and, despite the interesting opening sequence, is another straight-ahead track written in the radio-friendly style that had now become a Rainbow trademark. The same can be said for the next up, 'Fool For The Night'. It completes a trio of tracks at the beginning of the album that really highlight how Rainbow had opted for a sound based firmly in the centre ground of rock and were doing it well. Never a band to be too predictable, it is at this point that the album goes off on a tangent with 'Fire Dance'. It is a track that starts up sounding very much like the Rainbow of old and is a step away from the preceding three, arriving on the album at just the right point to inject a little more interest. 'Anybody There' slows it all down with a lovely instrumental piece by a typically precise and inspired Ritchie Blackmore. 'Desperate Heart' is artfully produced and as such raises the track into a well-constructed and standout track. 'Street Of Dreams' became the album's single but, despite it being a highlight on the album, sales were disappointing and the release only just managed to crawl into the top fifty. The position wasn't helped by the fact that the video accompanying the single was banned by MTV for its apparent hypnotic sequence. All in all it's a standout track on an album that, although having nothing obviously wrong with it, is equally not particularly remarkable. It has good production and good performances of good tracks and in a way that says it all: there is nothing truly outstanding in the whole thing. Even the trademark fireworks of Blackmore's solos are reduced despite the album clearly needing them. 'Drinking With The Devil' is a rock-solid piece of solid rock: nothing more, nothing less. The album then moves into another superb instrumental with Blackmore's rendition of 'Snowman'. On the face of it, the choice was a strange one with the original track from the animated film having been played to death. Needless to say, however, Blackmore's version has the touch of genius and is therefore altogether something special. It all comes to an end with 'Make Your Move' and with that track Rainbow all but signed off a fascinating and, to say the least, varied career as a studio band.

In March 1984 Rainbow played their final shows in Japan, complete with orchestra, and with the now-deafening rumours of a Deep Purple Mark II reunion abounding, the band was put on ice. Joe Lynn Turner, for one, was convinced and had even been told that the Purple reunion would only last an album and a tour, but that proved not to be the case; it would be a full 10 years before the Rainbow name was resurrected for one final time. Ironically, in late 1989 Joe Lynn Turner was brought in to fill the vocal spot with Deep Purple. The Purple reunion of Blackmore, Glover, Gillan, Paice and Lord was destined, of course, not to be without incident. In January 1985, Deep Purple with Blackmore back on guitar released the single 'Knocking At Your Back Door' from the album 'Perfect Strangers'. In amongst this, Rainbow's 1986 double live album 'Finyl Vinyl' came out and proved to be a fitting showcase for the many faces of Rainbow. It included some rare selections from the numerous variations of the Rainbow setup. In no particular logical order there are tracks sung by all three Rainbow vocalists spread over a six-year period; it acts as a more than worthwhile historical document of the various incarnations of the band. It was once again produced and re-mixed by Roger Glover. On the cover is the man in black himself sitting rather discontentedly on the side of the stage in front of a now-empty arena. The centre photographs, many of which were un-released until that point, had been taken throughout the Rainbow career. Many of Rainbow's tracks have been covered by other artists and Blackmore himself continues to perform versions of some Rainbow classics, such as 'The Temple Of The King', with his Blackmore's Night project.

Ritchie Blackmore also went on to appear on the 1987 Deep Purple album 'House Of Blue Light' and the following year's 'Nobody's Perfect', a live album recorded on tour. Trouble was soon looming, though, and during the next year Ian Gillan once again left the band. It was little surprise that one of the reasons highlighted was his continued clashing with Blackmore. As mentioned, Joe Lynn Turner, presumably tired of waiting for the Rainbow comeback, was brought in to add his vocal skills to the Purple camp who, in November 1990, subsequently released 'Slaves & Masters'. During this period Blackmore toured extensively with Deep Purple, criss-crossing the globe on numerous occasions. Further changes occurred in 1992 when their label RCA instigated Ian Gillan's return, thus ousting Joe Lyn Turner, for the appropriately named album 'The Battle Rages On', an altogether heavier, Gillan-influenced release. Of course it did exactly that, and by halfway through the band's European tour in 1993, discord within the band erupted once again when Blackmore made it clear that he was distinctly unimpressed by Gillan's performances and his tendency to forget the lyrics. The end was once again in sight, and Blackmore announced that he would once again be leaving Purple, this time for good, at the end of the European leg of the tour. Before leaving, in true Blackmore style, he was involved in an incident where he is shown throwing a glass of liquid over an onstage camera crew member before launching into a stupefying solo. The Japan leg was covered by the gifted Joe Satriani while a tired and emotionally drained Blackmore considered his next move.

That move turned out to be the temporary resurrection of Rainbow, and at the tail end of 1993 in New York, he began to hold auditions. By 1994 Rainbow's latest and last line-up would be complete and included ex-Praying Mantis singer Doogie White from Scotland; bass player Greg Smith, formerly with Alice Cooper, Blue Öyster Cult and Joe Lynn Turner; Paul Morris on keys; drummer John O'Reilly, who had previously been with Woodstock legend Ritchie Havens and, like Greg Smith, Blue Öyster Cult; and Joe Lyn Turner. Blackmore also recruited singer Candice Night, now of course very much a part of his life both at home and in Blackmore's Night. Writing quickly commenced and by early 1995 recording started on what would be Rainbow's last-ever album 'Stranger In Us All'. This was, if you excuse the pun, a purple patch for Blackmore, who was busy picking up numerous awards in Japan and Europe, having won various guitarist polls. The single from the album was 'Ariel', and once again it would gain plenty of airplay while the video was shown extensively on MTV. Of course any Rainbow line-up couldn't survive without changes, but this time the change of drummer back to Chuck Burgi, who had occupied the seat at the end of Rainbow's previous life, was forced on Blackmore rather than being one of choice. Just after the album was completed, John O'Reilly suffered a sports injury that kept him out of the subsequent tour. Burgi, of course, was an ideal replacement.

In fact, Greg Smith was not the first choice bass player for the new line-up either and was brought in after original selection, Rob de Martino, had left after only a few practice sessions. Already the changes were being rung. Doogie White had formed La Paz in his Scottish homeland before featuring in the more melodic Midnight Blue. In 1991 he fronted Praying Mantis and had also unsuccessfully auditioned for the vacant slot in Iron Maiden. White had also worked with ex-Rainbow drummer Cozy Powell. After Rainbow he worked with Yngwie Malmsteen and a band called White Noise. As we have seen, Greg Smith had a powerful pedigree, playing with the likes of Alice Cooper.

The line-up was set and work commenced on the album. To support the album the band, Blackmore along with White, Smith, Morris and Burgi, went to South America, where they played to sellout crowds in Brazil, Chile and Argentina and followed those triumphs with an equally successful European leg. John O'Reilly's misfortune in injuring himself as the tour commenced resulted in him leaving Rainbow, but he did work with Blackmore again a few years later when he performed with Blackmore's Night. Candice Night had also been recruited to provide backing vocals to this latest version of Rainbow and thereby began a lasting and productive relationship, both personal and musical, with Ritchie Blackmore.

Born in 1971 in Long Island, New York, Candice had occasionally supplied backing vocals to Deep Purple. Blackmore had also asked her to contribute to the lyrics for the new Rainbow line-up. Privately, they had been living together since 1991 and in 1994 announced their engagement. By the time Rainbow toured the States in February 1997, with new ex-Meatloaf drummer John Micelli on board replacing Burgi, who had moved on, they had already begun work on their new plans and formed Blackmore's Night, soon releasing their first album 'Shadow Of The Moon'. It sold spectacularly well, particularly in Japan and Germany, whilst announcing Blackmore's departure from the rock arena and into a field that had always interested and inspired him. To see him play live now, as in Paris 2006, with Blackmore's Night is to see a huge change not only in musical style but also in his apparent calmness and ease with the other band members and audience. He gives the impression of being a much more contented man away from the pressures of arena rock and performing music that he loves with the partner he also loves. On May 31st 1997 as 'Shadow Of the Moon' was selling well in Japan, Rainbow played to over 30,000 people at a festival at Esbjerg, Denmark. It was to be their last ever appearance. The Blackmore's Night album was released in Europe in June that year and Rainbow was finally laid to rest.

'Stranger In Us All' is therefore Rainbow's final studio album and contains several highlights that round off a career fittingly. Doogie White provides some really impressive vocals starting off with the album's first track 'Wolf To The Moon', a track that was written by Blackmore and White along with Candice Night's lyrics. Its title could be a track from a future Blackmore's Night album. All in all, it is a powerful opener and a solid reminder of what this band was still capable of. 'Cold Hearted Woman' comes next and is another Blackmore and White song. Given volume, this is another track well worthy of a Rainbow album. Another clean Blackmore break satisfies those hungry for his contribution and it is an altogether impressive opening. A different path is taken with 'Hunting Humans (Insatiable)', track three on the album, and once again White's voice is on top form. It is the longest track on an album of reasonably lengthy cuts at just under six minutes. It fades out wonderfully with Blackmore's distinctive style.

Ten years had passed since Rainbow last recorded any new material, but on the evidence of the first few tracks on this album, they managed to leave the fans in no doubt that they could still be a viable force. 'Stand And Fight' is a more standard rocker, but once again White covers it very well with some impressive vocal acrobatics. One of the album highlights arrives next with the single 'Ariel' written, significantly, by Blackmore and Night, a sign of the band to come. Lyrically rich and instantly likeable, it is a song of strength and subtlety with more than a touch of the east from Blackmore's ever-superb guitar. This would have sat well on, or even lifted, some of Rainbow's older albums and is a song that begins to show the promise in the new partnership of Blackmore and Night. It is a wonderful moment that ends with Candice Night's beautifully atmospheric vocals rounding off an altogether superb track.

Back to an altogether heavier track in 'Too Late For Tears', once again best played loud, the album displays a good balance with another strong track. It moves on with 'Black Masquerade': a track co-written by Blackmore, White and Morris and once again featuring the image-laden lyrics of Candice Night, it is a tapestry of all the old Blackmore influences put together to produce a track very representative of Rainbow's finer moments. Had their new Renaissance project not consumed both Blackmore and Night, it is quite clear that this line-up would have had quite a bit more mileage and potential left in it.

'Silence' opens with anything but and has a memorably powerful Blackmore riff. Doogie White once again, as he does throughout the whole album, proves his mettle with some great vocals. It is a powerful end to the Rainbow written material. It goes without saying that yet another fine example of Blackmore's guitar ends the track and leaves you wondering whether there is anything that this man cannot play; that is especially the case with the next track, a re-arranged version, by Blackmore and Night, of 'The Hall Of The Mountain

King'. Herein lies a key to the Blackmore dilemma: he could have gone in any direction he chose, but having taken Rainbow through the sometime commercialism during its previous life, it is clear that more atmospheric music such as this really excited him. His constant referrals to classical and Renaissance music, apparent throughout his incredible ongoing career, ultimately led to him going the whole distance by forming Blackmore's Night, and why not? Through his name alone along with the quality of musicianship that Blackmore demands and his calming partnership with Candice Night, he has brought the music he loves forward towards the masses.

The album ends with a superbly rousing re-make of 'Still I'm Sad' and effectively sounds out Rainbow's career. The album is strong and satisfying, and the line-up works on all levels. It is such a shame that Doogie White didn't get another Rainbow album to show his ability off as on this evidence it could have been a very successful fusion. For Rainbow fans of all stages of their career, the album successfully brought the band back into the light for a few short years. The album cover would seem to depict a Blackmore well into the transition from rock god to Renaissance-playing minstrel and his future much-maligned career in Blackmore's Night.

Rainbow came to an end once one of the world's best guitarists finally followed his muse and in so doing left intact a reputation that was equally rewarding and frustrating. Being a man of so many talents, Blackmore trod part way up many different paths, taking Rainbow with him. Rainbow had provided him with exactly the vehicle he needed after the frustrations of Deep Purple. It had been a band that had acted as a channel for all his various musical inspirations and ideas and therefore provided us with a more-than-fascinating look into the mind of the one-time rock god Ritchie Blackmore. Subsequent to Rainbow, Blackmore's Night continue to go from strength to strength, taking Renaissance music out to the already committed and the curious. Their concerts are still attended by Purple and Rainbow fans keen to catch a glimpse of their hero Ritchie Blackmore, and he quite often delights them by performing differing versions of some of the classics of those eras. They have gone on to produce several strongly selling albums and perform to appreciative audiences. The rock media meanwhile still focus on the apparent loss of their guitar hero, not fully understanding why he made the move into an area he clearly loves after a career that reached a pinnacle with Rainbow. He has spent 40 years pleasing us all and surely has now more than earned the right to please himself.

This man has produced some of the most instantly recognisable riffs in rock history with the likes of 'Smoke On The Water', 'Black Night' and his instantly identifiable version of 'Since You Been Gone'. He can also produce such mysterious epics as 'Stargazer', 'Gates Of Babylon' and 'Eyes Of Fire'. He could drag our attention towards the classical, the mystical, the historic and the Eastern. He could change personnel in the band and always come up with a combination that worked. He could create a chemistry of writing and music that is surely second to none. He could frustrate and infuriate whilst giving the impression that he was just as capable of storming off the stage due to some sound problem as he was of taking it by storm. Whatever Ritchie Blackmore turns up, the result is memorable. The man is unquestionably a legend demanding respect and if he wants to abandon a career in rock and sit on bales of straw playing the lute with his partner Candice Night to the delight of his now more modest following, he has earned every right to do just that. One thing is for certain: he will not be doing it half-heartedly; that is the one criticism that can never be levelled against him. With the Rainbow catalogue, he has left us with a rich legacy and one that will be there to enjoy because of and in spite of all things that make up the complex character Ritchie Blackmore.

RAINBOW IN THEIR OWN WORDS

Post-Purple: Ritchie Blackmore's Rainbow

Jon Tiven, Circus, September 1975 *(© Jon Tiven 1975)*

He is famed for cultivating a public image that extends beyond even the bounds of the antisocial. Even with Deep Purple, his own band, his relationship always seemed to be teetering on the brink of total alienation. Every week some new rumour would emerge as to who he was currently playing with, who he wasn't speaking to. Because of the glut of gossip, though, coupled with the fact that he seemed to be getting on reasonably well with the current Purple outfit, no one paid particular attention to rumours of Ritchie Blackmore's impending exit.

But it was no wolf call. For the first time ever, Ritchie has actually left the world's most successful metalloid rock band to have a go with Blackmore's Rainbow, a hard-hitting group with one album under their belt. Blackmore's decision is a landmark for several reasons — this is the first time a member of Deep Purple has left the band on good terms with the rest of the individuals. Blackmore's Rainbow (on Warner Brothers) is the first record Ritchie's ever made with total control over the direction, and it's the first album he's made since Machine Head that knocks his socks off. "I think you'll like it," he assured Circus Raves' six-string maniac, "it's got lots of guitar."

Blackmore's Rainbow wasn't anything more than a spare time solo album for Ritchie at first. The guitarist had every intention of staying with Deep Purple as usual, despite the rumours that he wasn't getting along with the group and wasn't too pleased with the music. "I think Stormbringer was all right, but Purple's always been best onstage," Ritchie said, "and you know me, I'm never happy with my music." At the time Ritchie was no less content with Purple's music than he'd ever been, it's just that he went out to make a casual piece of music, it turned into something far beyond what he'd expected, and the man merely decided that he'd be happier pursuing the road to Blackmore's Rainbow.

Contrary to what you might hear on the street, Ritchie is still on very good terms with the rest of Purple, unlike the situation with people who have left the group in the past. Roger Glover is off on his own, producing several groups, and hasn't talked to Ritchie in years; Ian Gillan has metamorphosed into quite the businessman, running his own recording studio, and doesn't have much to do with the Purple gang at all. And as for those who left the original group — Ritchie has an interesting story to tell.

"We just got over a court thing with our old bass player, Nicky Simpler. He sued us because we sacked him, he thought he was the fifth Beatle and just couldn't take it. I felt sorry for him in a way because he literally had nightmares about the whole thing for years — it was a bit heavy. Anybody else would've gone, 'Right, I'll show you what I can do on my own', that's the attitude I'd have if somebody kicked me out of a band."

But things are quiet now between Ritchie and Purple — Jon Lord and Ian Paice are auditioning new guitarists.

And Ritchie is holed up in California rehearsing the new band for a tour of America, which should commence any time now, showcasing Blackmore's Rainbow in medium-sized concert halls.

It didn't take them a long time to complete the album, but there was one little balls-up which kept the band from starting rehearsals for a while. "We left out three lines on Man on a Silver Mountain, the first track on the album (the single as well). It wasn't until we heard it back that we realised it, and it was the hook line of the song so we couldn't just let it be. We went all the way to Jamaica to add the line, and then we couldn't do it because the studio wasn't too hot and they booked us in for the wrong day, so we had to journey all the way to Munich. We were travelling around in clothes we had on because we thought we'd only be away for a day — it ended up taking us ten days."

A lot of people will be surprised at the finished product. The odd thing is that Rainbow isn't a total metallic attack of Strat power, but contains several pieces of evidence to the fact there is a sombre, melodic and peaceful side to the mysterious musician. It's hardly your archetypal guitar-flash-goes-solo album (Robin Trower and Paul Kossoff producing good examples of the latter). "I wanted to make it a group thing," says Ritchie, "although I think it'll appeal to guitarists. I've been listening to it a lot, which is something I never do — I like the record an awful lot."

The opening cut on Blackmore's Rainbow is every bit a rocker. Man on a Silver Mountain features music by Ritchie and words written by singer Ronnie Dio. "It's supposedly about some guy on top of a mountain who's like a Jesus Christ, it's kinda religious in a way. My interpretation is that some guy goes on top of a silver mountain, finds the silver, and realises that he can't get down again. It's vaguely a classical progression with about twenty-five chords in it, but you don't realise it because they're all relative, and it resolves after about thirty bars. It's one of my favourite numbers, very much like a Purple thing: what we call the 'Bagshot Bullet' guitar playing, Bagshot being where I come from. We recorded the album in a hotel, and it was really loud... I had one of the speakers down in a cellar to get echo on one side, and this was reverberating throughout the whole hotel so everybody was complaining."

But there's another side to Ritchie Blackmore's composing side, a pensive, quieter musical facet of his personality typified in the 'title track' called Catch the Rainbow. It begins with a Hendrixian guitar lick, and builds into a beautiful song which Ritchie himself compares to Jimi Hendrix's Angel.

"It's about ships of wonder and chains made of steel (from Sheffield), and our vocalist who wanted to be blessed at the time. That's why we had a vicar in on the sessions, we had this vicar walking around blessing everybody. That's why you'll hear Ronnie singing 'I want to be blessed all the time'. I think he actually did get blessed at one point. The vicar played bass on one of our sessions as well."

"What's his name?" I asked, chomping at the bit.

"That's a secret."

Which brings us to the question of how the group got its name, and the answer obviously isn't from a popular song of the fifties.

"The Rainbow is a club in LA where we'd congregate for joviality and wickedness of the first order. We liked the name, and I'd rather have left it as simply 'Rainbow,' but then again I wanted to get it across to the Purple fans that I was involved. I suppose my name means more to the public. I hope to eventually drop the Blackmore out of the title — I hate to be held responsible in case we release a record that's pure shit."

"But Ritchie, you do like the new album, don't you?"

"Hell, yes," he admits, "I'm playing it all the time. It's the most satisfying LP I've done since Machine Head and In Rock. With those albums, I really felt like I was doing something, and on this album I feel the same. To me, it's my third album," confessed the axeman, heard round the world on over a dozen albums.

"I'm quite pleased with my guitar playing — I got very excited by Ronnie's voice. Not that I'm ripping up and down the fingerboard all the time, but I'm playing well, getting off on his singing, and vice versa."

As opposed to the Purple method of renting a rehearsal studio, jamming for a week or two, and then laying down the tracks in a recording studio shortly thereafter, Blackmore's Rainbow decided to tackle the project of making a record in a far more premeditated fashion. Ritchie and Ronnie would get together at Ritchie's house and write the songs together, utilising just sheets of paper, a tape recorder, and, of course, a guitar or two.

"I'd usually put down some chords and ask which ones Ronnie'd prefer, he'd pick one set, and we'd take it from there. He'd always write the lyrics — sometimes I'd give him a vague melody but most of the time the melodies came from him. He's got an uncanny knack for writing melodies over nonsense."

Then again, there are songs like Snake Charmer which have been running around in Ritchie's head for quite a while, and actually sprang from a third source.

"Ian Broad, my best friend, thought up the title. Ronnie wrote a whole bunch of things around the title, and several parts had been written years ago. A lot of people might think it's the weakest track on the LP, but I liked it — with the guitar/voice thing it's really strong, and the three guitars sound fine together. It was a hard one to mix, as there's so much going on."

Now one of the last things you'd expect on a Ritchie Blackmore creation is a send-up of the Rolling Stones, but you can hear his exercising (or exorcising, as the case may be) his Keith Richards arthritic left hand on the most entertaining If You Don't Like Rock 'n' Roll (It's Too Late Now).

"We did it as a tongue in cheek thing about rock 'n' roll, we wanted an out-and-out rock 'n' roll thing so I thought this one up and figured, we could get it done in about half an hour and rip it down because it was so simple. You would not believe the hassles we went through to get it right — because it was so simple, nobody could play it. It became one gigantic headache, and in the end it took us two days to get it perfect."

And if you think that's fairly ridiculous, check out Self Portrait, which Ritchie describes as being a cross between Bach's Jesu, Joy of Man's Desire and Hendrix's Manic Depression. Or their extraordinary version of

Black Sheep of the Family, a song written by some members of a group called Quartermass and previously recorded by Chris Farlowe, which had to be recorded several times in three different locations to get the drum track correct. There's enough variety on this album to keep the listener wondering, 'Where the hell do Ritchie Blackmore's Rainbow think they're going? Everyone in the Purple organisation (who were the only people who had heard the album at the time this article was composed) has a favourite track, and they rarely seem to coincide.

For example, their booking agent, Bruce Payne, a long time friend of Ritchie's, likes Temple of the King very much.

"I was inspired to write that one by a programme on the television called Yoga for Health. I do Yoga, you know," Ritchie grinned. "Anyway, I was watching this television programme and liked it, and put it down on my tape recorder for future reference, not taking it seriously but just for a laugh. And then when I played it back a few days later it sounded pretty good. There are two classical guitars on that and one electric, but the electric guitar on that isn't really audible. It's got a medieval progression and a string ensemble/mellotron thing in the middle. There's a lyric in there, 'In the year of the fox' which I wanted to be changed to 'In the year of the badger', because I like badgers myself. A lot of people like that one, a lot of older people like it because it's more mellow, it's not a full-fledged assault on the ears. But I don't like to do more than one or two songs like that per album. We probably won't perform that onstage, because the vocal harmonies are very strange in the middle part — I don't think it's a proper stage number, we'd have everyone falling asleep.

"My favourite rock track on the album is Sixteenth Century Greensleeves. It was written by Robin Hood of Sherwood Forest. I went to the door one night and there was an arrow in the door holding a piece of paper, and it had this song written on it. There was a note attached reading 'Please record this song or I'll shoot you'. My favourite all-time song is the old tune Greensleeves, and in England I used to live just a little way from Windsor Castle. I was always up there just looking at the place. We wanted to record a song about castles and crossbows, and I was pleased that we were able to keep that hard rock thing within a classical mode. Hugh McDowell plays cello on that one (he being from the Electric Light Orchestra) and this is what our music is all about, really, Henry VIII and all his friends."

The next Blackmore outing, in a nutshell — Blackmore's Rainbow – combines medieval music and a 1975 spirit. Onstage you'll see them performing most of the tunes from the album, several new songs by Ritchie and Ronnie, and some songs written by outsiders that they just enjoy playing ("... but no Purple

Photo: Andre Csillag / Rex Features

material!" Ritchie insists). Purple are on their own now, Ritchie's off in another direction, and Blackmore's Rainbow is due to float across America soon. Only one thing will be the same — Ritchie will be retaining his spot at the right hand side of the stage. "I can only move to the left, I'm a bit spastic that way." Blackmore fans, keep that in mind when you start buying tickets to their shows, which should be pretty soon.

Rainbow Rising:
Ritchie Blackmore Gets It Up

Jon Tiven, Circus, 1 June 1976 *(© Jon Tiven, 1976)*

"**We've got The Rash from Stamford, Connecticut,**" reveals Mr Ritchie Blackmore, "**we've got Cozy Powell, the finest non-professional driver in England. Not to mention me, the Bagshot Bullet — we're the World's Top Band. Without a Country.**"

Between living in the California Sun, recording in German Studios, being managed by parties in both London and New York, you might say that Blackmore's Rainbow have that 'International Feel'.

As for the new album, Rainbow Rising — the first actual record featuring the group as a whole — you will find no split allegiances, lack of singular direction, or other divisive features. What you will find is 'straight ahead' rock music in the Ritchie Tradition. "Jon Lord loved it when he heard it," says Ritchie, speaking about his old companion from the Deep Purple days. "And Bruce Payne, our manager, thought it was the logical successor to Machine Head. You'll probably like it a lot. After all, it is the best thing I've ever done."

"But Ritchie," I interjected, "isn't that what you told us last time?"

"Well," said Ritchie rationally, "you always think you're bettering yourself. When you're in the studio you always think that it's the best thing you've ever done. It's only a matter of opinion, and I like my opinion. Everybody

79

who's heard it thinks it's my best playing in a long while. I suppose that's a compliment. What do they know?"

Rainbow Rising comes on strong in the visual department as well, packaged within a painting of a giant hand coming out of the ocean bringing forth a rainbow. "It looks a bit like something that would be done by Gustave Doré," says Ritchie, "a famous French painter. It was done by a bunch of people, including the person who did the windows on Led Zeppelin's Physical Graffiti."

Ritchie's a man concerned with such things, and the last album's cover was blown up as a backdrop for the band. "We'll be using this one on the tour as well, so we'll have two backdrops in addition to our Rainbow." Those who attended shows on Rainbow's first American tour can testify to the flash power and visual dynamics of their presentation.

And as for the record itself, Mr Ritchie Blackmore, ace reporter, interviewed lead singer Ronnie Dio about the contents of Rainbow Rising's lyrics, throwing in his own two cents all the while. The results of said discussion are as follows:

Blackmore: Tarot Woman kicks off the album, something about a lump who reads cards, predicts the future and all this business. True?

Dio: I recall it was originally called something else, but yes, that's the basic story behind Tarot Woman. The main character is told by this 'Tarot Woman' that a chick is going to fuck him over; she tells him to beware a smile and a bright and shiny face. Ritchie, are you interested in this jazz?

Blackmore: It scares me to death, but it's really true.

Dio: It frightens me as well. I'd sink my faith into palmistry.

Blackmore: That's a fast rocker, but what about Run with the Wolf? Does that have anything to do with the Bad Company song of similar title?

Dio: Certainly not, no Bad Company here. It is a heavy song set in a Transylvanian pub.

Blackmore: I don't know what their song is about, and I don't know what ours is about either.

Dio: I don't want to reveal any secrets, so let me merely quote a few lines: "In the light of the day/You can hear the old ones say/Was that sound last night the wind?/Can you feel the change begin?/By the fall of the snow a single soul will go with footsteps on the white/There's an unholy light! Something evil passing by/What's to come when the siren calls you go to Run with the Wolf." Not bad, huh? How would you characterise the next song, Mr B?

Blackmore: Starstruck is a mildly amusing tale. It's all about this lump named Muriel who's been following me all around Europe for the past few years, a real lunatic. We play a concert in Paris and she'd be there without fail, then we'd fly to Lyon and she'd be at the airport waiting for our plane to arrive. One day I looked outside my window and thought I saw one of my bushes move through my garden. I kept watching, and sure enough she'd found my house so I set my dogs on her. They're not mean or anything, just scary. One tried to have a go at her just as we pulled them away. And that's only the second to the last song on Side One.

Dio: Lest we not forget the two minutes and 59 second song closing out the side which puts, the rhetorical question, Do You Close Your Eyes (When You're Having a Go)?

Blackmore: And do you, Our Dee?

Dio: Err... I do.

Blackmore: I've been told by several people that it should be the single. It's got that hook that the postman can whistle as he does his rounds. It's a very simple rock tune that the public'll take to, although it's not wholly representative of where the band is at. Then again, Side Two is comprised of two nine-minute tracks, and I'm not sure that this is where the band is at either.

Dio: And which songs are these, pray tell?

Blackmore: Who's interviewing who, small fry? Stargazer features a 42-piece orchestra, mellotron, and a string thing all playing this half-Turkish scale. This is my favourite track of the lot. Then there's Light in the Black, very fast rock 'n' roll — about nine minutes of madness and solos. The drums are heavy-sounding, in fact they are all through the album. What the hell are those lyrics about, Mr D?

Dio: Stargazer is written from the standpoint of a slave in Egyptian times. He is serving The Wizard, who observes the skies and stars and becomes obsessed with the idea of flying. The slaves are building a tower of stone so The Wizard can jump off the top and take to the air. Finally this Wizard, this Stargazer, attempts to fly and, of course, falls to his death. The slaves arc released, and this is where the song Stargazer ends, and Light in the Black begins. The Wizard has died and the slaves are free, but all they've known all their lives is an allegiance to the Stargazer. They don't know where to turn or what to do until they see the Light in the Dark. I think that about covers the album, Ritchie.

Indeed it does. As stated previously in the text, this is the first album by the group as such, for the last Rainbow album featured only Ritchie, Ronnie, and a cast of individuals quick to fade into rock 'n' roll obscurity. The new members — Cozy, Jimmy and The Rash (Tony Carey) — have not only been able to gel as a band, but retain their distinctive playing styles as well. Cozy Powell (on drums) is perhaps the most famous of the new members, having made his reputation alongside Jeff Beck, Donovan, and Hot Chocolate, as well as doing a Top 20 single (worldwide) under his own name.

"Cozy's worked out well," admits Ritchie, "we didn't do very much editing at all because he insisted on recording everything straight through. A lot of times a band will go into the studio and do a longer song in sections, because you can throw in everything you want knowing you only have to play 180 bars. If you do a long thing straight through, you worry about making a mistake and you tend to hold back. We only had one edit, which is quite astounding considering that Side Two has two nine-minute songs on it."

"Cozy's a lot of fun. We go out racing on the throughway, Cozy drives while I watch out for the cops. This one time we were racing at 110mph when I spotted a cop car, Cozy had us slowed down to 55mph by the time we met. They stopped us, and we were all tense waiting for their reaction… they got out of their car, laughing, came over to us and said, 'nice brakes'."

The Rainbow Tour takes the group all over the US of A, 40 cities in two months, getting off just in time for Ritchie, Ronnie, Cozy, Jimmy, and Tony to catch their shares of bicentennial summer celebrations. It'll be rest and recuperation from hard playing and occupational diseases, this being a trek to rival those of Purple's Golden Days.

"It's going to be a long, hard, silly tour," Ritchie bitches. "The bad thing about these tours is that after about ten gigs all the equipment is broken, everybody's got to work twice as hard just to compensate for the technical problems, and you've still got 30 cities to play. If I have to put out extra it's tough enough, but if it's not going to look and sound any good regardless, that's a drag."

Ritchie Blackmore — the eternal optimist — probably complains about the room service if his toast is a wee bit cold. Yes, it's a hard life for these ill-paid, downtrodden workhorses of the music industry who play Trilby by day and Galahad by night. Yet, there are times when it all seems worthwhile. The band was off in Munich, recording, and during their free time they decided to go off ice-skating. There was a band playing at the rink, and Ritchie's boys were skating around the rink when all of a sudden one member of the group came upon a brilliant suggestion. As they rounded the bandstand, on Ritchie's cue they all leaped into the band pit, grabbed the instruments away from the musicians, and proceeded to run through a few numbers.

"Everyone was shocked at first," Ritchie comments, "but most of them knew who we were we're

Photo: Pictorial Press

quite well-known in Germany — and they sat down and watched us play the Ice-Skating Blues. We stayed up there for an hour, and then just handed the guitars back to the band, jumped into the rink and resumed skating. It's the first time I've played in ice-skates, and I must say it was enjoyable. Good fun." Indeed.

Ronnie James Dio at Rainbow's End

Don Snowden, LA Vanguard, March 1976 *(© Don Snowden, 1976)*

"**I**'m going to try to be drunk by the time these are over, you know that?" Ronnie James Dio commented as he cracked open another bottle of Michelob. The diminutive lead singer, lyricist and composer of Rainbow, the band Ritchie Blackmore formed after his departure from Deep Purple, is in the midst of a hectic schedule of promotional activities following the completion of a two month American tour that focused on cities not normally hosting a large number of rock concerts.

Dio first caught the ear of the semi-legendary guitarist during several tours where Elf, Ronnie's former band, performed as the opening act for Purple. Ironically, the element that brought together the creative forces behind a group that easily falls into the heavy metal category was their collaboration on a piece (16th Century Greensleeves) based on medieval music.

"I started musically when I was seven years old," Ronnie related. "I was a trumpet player. I played in orchestras, in concert bands. Playing that kind of music, it gave me an insight into classical music: how it was constructed, why it was constructed, and I got a real liking for it. I got interested in medieval modes, in a simplistic Allan O'Dale kind of way who would just go around the countryside being the minstrel. That was very soothing to me. My thought was always, 'If I could put that kind of a concept together with hard, aggressive rock 'n' roll, that would be a really unique and original step.' Well, as luck had it, the two people who were thrown together, Ritchie and I, had exactly the same ideas."

But there is little evidence of that classical orientation to be found on the surface of Rainbow's live presentation. Their performance at the Starlight Amphitheatre was marred by a surprising reliance on metallic clichés and a seemingly interminable succession of breakdowns to feature solo spots by individual members on their instruments.

"I'm not a very religious person," he cautioned. "I have no concept of what a God is; it may be the man on the silver mountain. My image of the man on the silver mountain is a guy with flowing robes and lightning coming from his fingertips, kind of a mythological figure like Zeus. The song is more of a plea from the fallen and to the fallen that there is hope, I will make you holy again. Ask me and I will do something for you."

Over the course of the conversation, the image of Dio that gradually comes into focus is that of a small town boy brought up on traditional American (and probably Catholic) virtues. Cockiness and a competitive spirit mingle with self-consciousness as he strains to convey the points he wants to get across. But visions of the all-American boy clash repeatedly with the lyrical themes of many of Ronnie's songs, most notably Run with the Wolf (werewolves, vampires and the like) and Stargazer, the eight minute drone epic from the Rainbow Rising LP built around a story of wizards and slaves.

"I always wanted to write a song about a very oppressed person," Dio said, in explaining how he wrote Stargazer. "To me the most oppressed person I could think of was a slave, more or less in Egyptian times, who was always led around by chains, whipped, and never had an identity. I wanted to write it from the standpoint of the slave and then have the slave, through his eyes, give you his impression of The Wizard, who doesn't seem to have feet, who has a big long flowing robe. I picture The Wizard's eyes being totally turned back so he has no pupils.

"So here's this totally oppressed individual," he continued, "who's speaking not only for himself, but for all the other slaves around him, and he still believes that The Wizard will take them all out of this oppression and lead them to his star. At the end of it, he climbs up to the top of the pyramid, this tower of stone that took them nine years to build. He launches himself off the top of the tower and there's total silence as he falls instead of rises, and they still believe until they see splat! and he's just a little lump of blood on the sand."

"It correlates itself with the way almost all of the people in this country believed in Richard Nixon up until the time he decided he was going to take a leap off the tower and fell flat on his ass and became just a little lump of blood and putty. That was my way of saying that the common man will always rise above the leader who oppresses them. I don't feel that you can ever give social comment without making it a fable in some way, of having a little story that keeps the interest.

Hi, I'm Ritchie Blackmore. And I want to tell you what I've been doing for the past fifteen years...

Jon Young, Trouser Press, July 1978   *(© Jon Young, July 1978)*

As Dave Schulps and I rolled along in the darkness to our impending interview, we were filled with apprehension. After all, Ritchie Blackmore has never been known as a pussycat. In fact, most accounts of his years with Deep Purple emphasise his moodiness, sullenness, and even outright hostility. The Teutonic severity of Ritchie's current group, Rainbow, does little to suggest that time had mellowed Blackmore the least bit. We didn't even know where we were being driven! What if Ritchie got annoyed with our questions and had us 'silenced'? Paranoia strikes deep.

There was nothing to worry about, as it happened. After a circuitous drive we pulled up to a suburban bar in Greenwich, Connecticut (Ritchie lives nearby), and parked ourselves in a greasy-looking swinging singles place. Over a typically giddy bar room roar, interrupted occasionally by notes from an 'admirer' who asked things like 'are you Deep Purple?' we had our talk.

Ritchie Blackmore turned out to be a genial model of decorum, and was fully prepared to discuss anything. Indeed, when we got over the surprise of discovering him to be a pleasant fellow, he even fielded borderline tactless questions, unthinkable to ask of someone with his image. My only complaint about the thoughtful and open Mr Blackmore was that he insisted on keeping his juiciest comments off the record. Rainbow had that evening finished a rehearsal prior to their multi-month tour in support of a new album, Long Live Rock 'n' Roll.

Seeing as how this was the band's fourth album, why the long wait to try and make a mark on America?

"It's just that the other markets came first, Europe and all that. We took advantage of it rather than just playing around America as a small time band. Now the only market left is America and we're the underdog. Most of the time we're sharing the bill with REO Speedwagon and Foghat is topping the bill in other places. It's not like starting again. A lot of people feel that, but it's just something you do. I'm quite looking forward to it. It means I can get back to the bar afterwards. If you're a top-billed act you get back to the hotel and everything's closed."

Did Deep Purple audiences get too big?

"They were too big sometimes. It was moving too fast. It's funny how sometimes it will escalate and turn into something that big, when you know you're just the same as any other band. All these people are turning out to see this band and next year they'll be turning out to see some other band equally as bad or as good, whichever way you look at it. The way it's been going I think it's been getting worse. In America you have some very strange big groups."

Like Kiss?

"No, Kiss I like because they don't care what people think of them. They take a chance and it's worked. They're the first ones to admit they're not good musicians. I'm talking about middle of the road bands that turn out that lethargic, laid back cocaine beat. The DJs love it and they play and play it all the time."

Oh, Fleetwood Mac?

Laughing, "Funny you should mention them. Nice people, but I have reservations about what they're doing. But the rest of America doesn't seem to have reservations. It's gone into this mellow thing and I'm not keen on that. I like intense music that comes across as drama, as acting."

The new wave has that excitement, doesn't it?

"Well, it's got the impetus, the energy, but it hasn't got the music. That's wrong as well. I don't quite know what I prefer to listen to, the new wave or Fleetwood Mac. I often think of that and I think I would play Fleetwood Mac because I can't take the other stuff."

To go back to square one, when did you start guitaring?

"When I was 11. It mostly was my idea along with my father. He made sure I went along to proper lessons, because if I'm gonna have a guitar, I've got to learn it properly."

Did you have it in your mind to rock?

"Yeah, because there was a guy called Tommy Steele prancing around with a guitar and Presley and all that

Photo: Pictorial Press

lot. I wanted to do that just like everybody else… Duane Eddy, then Hank B. Marvin, then Django Reinhardt, Wes Montgomery, James Burton, Les Paul. I bought all of Les Paul's records up until I was about 17, but after that I didn't have any idols. Then I was mostly practising. I listened to rock via Buddy Holly up until 16, 17 (1962). Then I was on my own. I didn't have any inspiration from guitarists, it went more into inspiration from violinists. I don't listen to too much rock 'n' roll, really. Jimi Hendrix was good and I liked Cream. I wasn't really getting off on people like the Beatles and the Hollies, all that vocal business. The Stones? I considered them idiots. It was just a nick from Chuck Berry riffs. Chuck Berry was OK. Sometimes I'm outspoken, but I don't have any time for the Stones. I can see why they're respected and their rhythms are very good, very steady on record. I respect them but I don't like them."

And the blues?

"It might sound condescending but I find them a little too limited. I like to play a blues when I'm jamming, but then I want to get on to other things. I listened to BB King for a couple of years but I like singers more than guitarists. Albert King I thought was a brilliant singer. That depth, which comes out in Paul Rodgers, too. I do like a blues base to some things, that can be very interesting with classical overtones."

So what was your professional gig?

"My first band was with Screaming Lord Sutch. He had amazing publicity stunts — he would go up to the Prime Minister and stick his hand out and say 'hello there.' The Prime Minister's first reflex was to shake his hand and suddenly he's thinking 'who is this man?' He's got pictures of him about to shake hands with everyone in the business. He used to copy Screamin' Jay Hawkins.

"From there I was onto a group called the Outlaws. I did sessions for three years. They were known as a very steady band, good for session work, so we used to work together for sessions (besides putting out a number of singles of their own). You were just given the music to play, sometimes it was just the backing tracks. It wasn't our job to know who we were playing for, it was just to get the money and go."

Did you read music?

"Yeah, but not well. It was more like chord sheets. Pagey was in all those sessions. Sometimes you'd get complete rock 'n' rollers who could play but wouldn't be able to read and others who could read but wouldn't be able to improvise. Sometimes they'd want rock 'n' roll sessions and that's what we'd do."

You and Jimmy Page both played in Neil Christian's band, right?

Blackmore laughed and mused a second before answering: "I was with him on and off for about a year. Chris, that's his real name, was a slightly bizarre person to work for. In fact, Jimmy Page played with him for about three years. That's when I first met Pagey. I was 16 years old. He was good then; I rate him as a three dimensional guitarist. He has a range, he has ideas, but he can't be everything, so sometimes he lacks on improvisation a bit. He's so caught up with producing and everything else concerned with being a top band, whereas someone like Jeff Beck is entirely in the opposite direction. Jeff can extemporise really well, but I don't think he can write a song. It's always somebody else's tune. He doesn't have many ideas, but he's a brilliant guitarist.

Our brief search for other three dimensional guitarists failed to turn up any more that met with Blackmore's approval. Ritchie was asked to evaluate himself.

"This is gonna sound very cocky, but I think I can improvise better than any rock guitarist. My failing is composing, I really fall down in composing. I can come up with riffs and I'm good at improvising, but I'm not very good at putting a song together. I have done, because there's nobody else around to do it anyway. I feel very frustrated in my songwriting. I think it's terrible half the time. But improvising for me is no problem — in fact, it's something I could do all the time. That might sound slightly weird."

So you tend not to memorise your parts.

"No, that's partly my downfall. I have a very bad technical memory, so I can't remember, if I write a tune, exactly what the notes are. It's really exasperating, 'cos I'll write one and, 'That's great, I'll play it again and record it'. And I'll play it again and, 'Oh dear, I've forgotten it. What did I play?' It's really annoying. I don't like to write. It's a chore for me. I do it because there aren't a lot of other people around me who do it. It's not knocking the people around me… songs are a letdown half the time."

But didn't you do most of Purple's music?

"I did most of the riffs and progressions because, basically, we had so many arguments in the first two years of Purple, and I was sick of it, so I said, 'Let's split it five ways', because everyone was bickering about, 'I wrote that one note'… 'Include this song which is a bunch of rubbish, but I wrote it'. Every band goes through that. There's one thing today we haven't got over with modem technology. We haven't found a way to fashion a computer to take the information and tell you who's written the song. That would be very nice.

"People said to me, 'You were silly to split it five ways for most of it,' but I said, 'Purple wouldn't have been together at all if I hadn't done that,' because they were very strong-minded people. It would have died out in 1970 if I hadn't done that. They did (write) to a certain extent, but not to the extent that they should have gotten a fifth share on every song. Jon (Lord) would have written what would have been one song an LP, but he would get out of eight songs a fifth share on each song. It's the only way to work. But to give him his due, the drummer (Ian Paice) gave his enthusiasm, Jon was always there for stability. He wouldn't come up with the ideas, but he'd remember them when I forgot them. Ian (Gillan) would write the lyrics, and Roger (Glover) used to write some."

How did Deep Purple get together?

"I saw Ian with another band in Hamburg in 1967 and I said 'when I get something I'll let you know'. When this Purple thing came up, I said, 'Right, we've got something here'. We had a millionaire backer (Chris Curtis, of Searchers fame) — it's very hard to start without financial backing. He just wanted a very good group. As far as he was concerned Jon was the best organist he knew and I was the best guitarist… but once we all got together he kind of fell out. I told Jon about Ian and then we got the other two. Jon knew Nick (Simper) and I knew Rod (Evans) the singer. We were all living in one big mansion in England which we used to rehearse in. There were a lot of things happening there, psychic phenomena. For the first few years Purple had no direction whatsoever. If anything, we used to follow what Jon wanted to do, which was OK because nobody else had any ideas."

Be that as it may, Deep Purple roared into the American top five in the fall of 1968 with an acidy remake of Joe South's Hush. Yet that original band never seemed capable of capitalising on it. How come?

"Jeff Wald (Mr Helen Reddy) was our manager on the road and we did a lot of gigs that didn't mean anything. They were ballrooms, they weren't on the circuit to make it. The only time we really made it was when we supported Rod Stewart, supported him as we're doing now in order to do the right gigs and be seen. We'd be playing around, headlining all the wrong places. Nobody knew where to put us. We played with Cream at the Hollywood Bowl, but they never really knew who we were.

"I really admired Jimi Hendrix and I really loved Vanilla Fudge so we just tried to integrate the two. We did Hey Joe and a lot of standards because we didn't have a lot of writing going on. I'd never written a tune before '69 when I started feeling my way and came up with a few ideas. But at the time we were just so over the moon about playing with good musicians, because we'd had such a hard time finding good musicians. You find them and you ask someone to join — 'We've got a great band' — 'Yeah, sure, how much do I get?' — 'Well, it's only just rehearsals for the moment'. You know the story. We were just so pleased to be playing with each other that we didn't really care which direction we went in.

"Until about '70, when we decided we should replace the singer and bass player. The singer wanted to go anyway and the bass player was asked to leave." Ritchie's friend Micky Underwood (now with Strapps) was in the soon-to-be-defunct Episode Six, and he invited Ritchie to come down and check out their singer, Ian Gillan.

"Ian was amazing, his voice, the way he looked and everything else. Stupendous. We took him right there. We didn't know who to have on bass but Ian recommended Roger.

"Why we thought we had to change singers was because of Robert Plant. We were playing at Mother's in Birmingham and Robert got up to sing with Terry Reid. We thought 'Christ Almighty'. He was so dynamic. And the next two weeks we were looking for a singer, people who had Robert Plant's dynamic approach. So it was thanks to him."

"Zeppelin, I liked their hard approach when they came out and did Whole Lotta Love. I immediately tuned in with that type of style because before when we were fiddling around with orchestras, I thought, 'Something's wrong, I'm not giving all that I can'. Thanks to them for the inspiration. They got it from Jeff Beck, who got it from the Small Faces…"

In Rock was the right formula: agile musicians playing with a tidal wave of force. But not a Zeppelin steal; the textures were much more varied, the sound more flexible. Suddenly escalating popularity soon led to "super group" status. That must have been a little surprising.

"I was surprised because I was happy to be working."

Did you like the Yardbirds?

"Well. Jeff was always brilliant. Yeah, I did like the Yardbirds very much. They were an exception. Jeff was one of the first to use distortion. There were quite a few guys before Jeff that used distortion but you wouldn't have heard of any of them. Like Bernie Watson with Lord Sutch. In 1960 he made a record with Cyril Davies which had an amazing solo, all distortion. It was like Hendrix on a good night. He now plays for the Royal Philharmonic. Just gave it all up."

Ritchie said he was motivated to try something like that himself in 1963. The results (I just freaked out) can be found on the B-side of the Outlaws' version of I Hear You Knockin'. Archaeologists and fans take note. From there, via You Really Got Me ("The solo was too bad to be Page. It had to be Dave Davies."), talk drifted to stealing.

"Everybody steals. It's healthy to steal. The thing is to disguise who you're stealing from. I used to steal a lot from Jimi Hendrix."

But Rainbow Eyes, on the new album, sounds especially like Jimi.

"What it is, is the inflection of playing in fourths. Jimi used to play a lot of fourths. After several single notes he'd play a fourth above and that gave him the effect. On Axis: Bold As Love it's all fourths."

Digress, digress. Some albums and many converts (and bucks) later, Purple found itself in a state of chaos after the recording of Who Do We Think We Are?

"I wanted to leave with Ian (Paice) at the time because we'd both had enough. I am a very sensitive kind of person, believe it or not. I was working too hard and couldn't take the strain. I had hepatitis and was in the hospital for a couple of months, which was a good rest for me; I needed it. I said the only way I would stay was if we completely changed the band. 'Get a new bass player and I'll stay'. Ian and Jon said OK. Glenn (Hughes from Trapeze) came in, so I stayed. Ian and I were gonna form another band with Phil Lynott from Thin Lizzy, actually."

What did this aborted group with Lynott sound like?

"It was like Hendrix number two. He looked like Hendrix, sounded like Hendrix. He was just singing, Roger was playing because he was a better bass player then." (More than a little odd to ask Glover along considering Blackmore insisted on throwing Glover out of Purple…)

With the guitar boom in full flower, wasn't there a temptation to do a solo LP? (This question came the closest of any to making Blackmore blow his cool.)

Scoffing a little and raising his voice, he said; "My solo LPs were Deep Purple! Because off the record…" The gist of his comments was that he felt he was doing too much of the work.

To kill off the Purple era (that drew a snicker from Ritchie) he was asked to rate the group's albums.

"My favorite LP would be Machine Head followed closely by In Rock and then Burn. Fireball I didn't like. Who Do We Think We Are? I haven't heard for ages. I didn't like it when we did it. We were having a lot of friction at the time, a hell of a lot. Ian (Gillan) was about to leave. I was sick to death of Ian, Ian was sick to death of me. Girlfriends were involved. I thought, 'Here we go again, another LP'. We'd had one week off the road then we were told to go into the studio and make another LP. It was just ludicrous, we didn't know what to do. I felt great about Burn (the first one with the new group) because we'd had a year to write it.

"See… In Rock, Fireball down, Machine Head up, Who Do We Think We Are? down, Burn up.

Stormbringer was on the wane. When we did Stormbringer I thought it was a very cold LP."

Had you decided to leave by the time of Stormbringer?

"Yeah, that's it, I thought, 'I wanna see what everybody else is doing, I'm tired of pushing the band'. Seven years is long enough, I thought the band was on the decline. There were other bands coming up. Jon was into drinking, wining and dining. Ian was into cars, expensive things."

But the new line-up had worked at first.

"It worked for the first year and then it started getting a little bit shaky. It started getting into this funky music. I can't stand it. I like it vicious."

Come Taste the Band, which featured Tommy Bolin on guitar and was the only post-Blackmore LP, seemed to lean in a Stevie Wonder direction.

"That's exactly where they were going and I wasn't interested in being around for that! I thought it was only proper of me to say, 'Look, I'm going. I don't want to break up the band but I'm off. Get another guitarist and do your thing'. I just didn't want to be around for all that cool pseudo… They were shocked. My music was up-front music, hate music. Their music was becoming much more like, 'If you don't like it just click your fingers'.

"I wanted to get out gracefully if I could. What I thought was just a matter of opinion. I thought, 'Now it'll be interesting to see because I'm not pushing my ideas. Let's see your ideas'. Which, whenever I said that in the studio they'd say, 'Oh, well, we don't have any ideas', or 'We're waiting to see what you think so we can collect the 20 per cent',but it sounds bitter to say that.

"I took a gamble because at that time I'd acquired enough money to say, 'I'm gonna take a chance and go out gracefully and maybe make a crash landing in something else. But I'm certainly not gonna go down with a big name band'. I could have stayed with Purple and earned a good living for five years, a steady kind of decline (laughs). But I wasn't interested. It was very cushy the last two years of Purple, everything was financed. They said, 'Do the California Jam'. I said, 'No'. 'You'll make half a million'. 'We'll do it'."

There were some stories of you demolishing cameras there.

"When I'm onstage I feel very hyper anyway and it was a combination of that and being very annoyed because they'd given us hell. They'd been so conservative about the whole festival. Everything was built around the fact that this was gonna be a festival for the benefit of the camera people from ABC. The kids that paid ten dollars each will not have any fun, but we don't care if they won't be able to see the band. That's beside the point as long as we get the money'.

"I said to my manager, 'I hope they're not gonna have a press enclosure'. I looked the next day and sure enough there was about 100 feet of just press who were bored stiff. The audience was about a hundred yards away so I insisted that they let the people who had paid into the press enclosure. I was going on getting madder and madder. All the kids were in the distance going 'yaaaa yaaaa' and the press were going, 'Oh boring, another loud metal rock 'n' roll band. Where's the beer?' You don't need that.

"I hate the business. I love the fans and I love the music. But I don't like the radio, I don't like the DJs, I don't like the press."

So why are you talking to us?

"Yeah, right. Well, you're buying this round, mate." (Ulp!)

So exit Purple and enter Rainbow, which is dominated by the twin howitzers of Ritchie and Cozy Powell, once with Beck, on drums. (Ronnie Dio is a good enough singer, but it would take the Mormon Tabernacle Choir to stand up to the volume of those two.)

"Cozy and I, we're always trying to outsmart each other. He's a very fast person, him with his cars. Me, with my medieval music, he hasn't got a clue where I'm coming from. So we have our differences, but when we're onstage we click because he wants to be the best drummer and I want to be the best guitarist.

"It works to a certain degree. Sometimes we do tend to get a little carried away with being very aggressive when we should slack it off. I find to record we should tone down everything. We have to mush it up a little, put some icing on it to make it sell."

"In Europe and Japan they're more into adrenaline, but in America they wanna hear safer things. I've never really studied American culture as far as music goes, but I've been listening more and more. We're gonna concentrate more on a backbeat. We'll be playing more slow songs. I know what the American people are looking for — I don't really care what the American DJs are looking for, they piss me off no end."

Jeez, shades of 'Radio Radio'! Just how far would you compromise?

"Not very far. I cannot play anything which is not in me. I could never play like Fleetwood Mac. I could play like that if I was fast asleep (chuckling). I'm not trying to be derogatory, I just cannot play that way. Lucky for them it's worked because they were going through some hard times about six years ago. So I'm glad for them as people. They're very nice people."

How do you feel about your audiences, seeing as how they tend to be so wild and crazy? It's hard to imagine that they catch too much of the music.

"In Purple I was happy to have any audience. In Rainbow I come offstage quite confused sometimes. There are certain numbers we do that are very intricate and I know they've missed them. But I can't expect them to catch on. They're not musicians, it's Friday night, they've finished their work, they want to have a good time, they want to see someone break a guitar (which he often does). I can't expect to educate people because if they'd wanted to become educated they would have become musicians themselves. At the same time I do like to listen to certain quiet parts that we play and get on to the party at the end. I don't understand an audience that's stomping all the way through and saying 'let's boogie man, let's get it on'."

So you do get upset.

"Yeah, I do a bit. I'll just stop or I'll go through the motions. 'We'll give you what you want'. Four-to-the-bar-stomp-stomp-stomp."

Ever considered playing another kind of music?

"Yeah, I have thought about that, but I'm very interested in extreme rock 'n' roll. At the other extreme, I'm interested in medieval modes, quiet fifteenth-century sitting in a park playing little minuets… I don't like to mix the two. I haven't reached the stage where I can play classical the way I'd like.

"I think I would miss the masses. Those type of people, they're extremely brilliant players, but they play in front of twenty people. There is that self-esteem thing that comes in, too. You do like to be proud of yourself and play in front of all these people, sharing something. If you're playing in front of 20 people you think it's a bit strange, what you're doing. You need a certain response. Five to ten thousand people is great, after that it becomes…"

What if Rainbow got really big?

"Well, I'm self-destructive. I would knock it on the head and start again. I love to play in Europe because they have seaters over there that are no bigger than eight thousand, ten thousand, and that's just right. You can still become intimate with the audience. In America things can get out of hand, as with Purple playing stadiums. I don't think I would want to do that again.

"You've got a manager coming along saying, 'Look, this is worth a lot of money. Think of what you can buy'. And you're thinking. 'Yeah, that's true'. You do the gig and you think, 'Oh dear, all those people have just heard me play a lot of nonsense'. But when you're faithful to the people and you say, 'Look, I've got something really honest to play to you, listen', they won't. When you're in front of 100,000 people and you're playing utter shit, because you're a cult figure or a name, they'll listen, because they've been told by their

Photo: Pictorial Press

friends to listen."

Does it ever bother you that you don't get more respect?

"In a way. I'm good. Some people know I'm good. Some people I want to know I'm good. I'm not into being a personality, a Johnny Carson, a Rod Stewart. I'm very thankful for as far as I've got, and I really don't think I should have any more than I have. If I hear other bands and I hear how bad they are, I get a little bit upset that people are buying their records in the millions. But I know my limitations. I think this is more than I deserve. I can't believe that people take as much notice of me as people do. I just think there's such a poor standard in rock 'n' roll. I think it's disgustingly low."

Rock isn't a musician's medium.

"No, but it should be. Because of its limitations rock 'n' roll is very difficult and classical is very closely related to rock 'n' roll. It's very disciplined; the modal structure is similar to rock. But I'm talking about progressive rock, not the Rolling Stones. When I play I always incorporate classical runs from violins and things like that."

So whatever happened to original Rainbow members Tony Carey (keyboards) and Jimmy Bain (bass)?

After a mysterious laugh, "Tony was a bit of a raver so he got a bit too heavy. He was asked to leave the first time and he was asked to come back. After a while he left of his own accord. He couldn't take the pressure. We were coming into contact with unforeseen psychic phenomena, which is kind of another story. It's just kind of a hobby of mine, psychic phenomena. He couldn't take that, 'cos we were playing at the Château in France. It got very heavy spiritually and he backed out. He thought I was completely mad. He thought I was trying to kill him. I don't know why he thought that." (Said with no irony.) "Jimmy Bain was a great guy, fantastic person, but his bass playing left a little bit to be desired."

How do you feel about your music being called heavy metal?

"It's better than punk, which means inferior. It suits us fine. I know I can play a bloody concerto any day, so it doesn't bother me at all. It would bother someone who was sensitive and knew their limitations."

By this time the hour was late and things were decidedly less businesslike. The pursuit of musically relevant info was soon abandoned for more speculative matters, as Blackmore reflected…

"Sometimes I feel like I own the stage completely on my own for an hour. I'm just going crazy. The adrenalin is so much that all my musical upbringing is thrown into intensity onstage rather than being a musician. After 22 years of playing it goes instead into a mood and comes out as an aggressive bulldozer. I don't know why, I often wonder why. I'm not an aggressive person offstage, I don't know why I am on."

Way back when, you used to say how rude you thought Americans are. Does that still hold?

"I've accepted America for what it is. The older I get, the broader my outlook on life gets. I can see why someone thinks this way or that. The one thing I think about Americans, I wish they would bring up their kids with a bit more discipline. Stop giving them hamburgers and shit like that. Stop pampering them. The mother and father seem to lay down their whole life for them. The kid takes over the whole family. I think it's disgusting."

What about the times we live in?

"I think we're going through a period now where nobody knows what's really going to happen in 25 years. This era will be written off as a group called the Rutles, or should I say the Beatles, and that's about it. We're just bordering on being invaded by UFOs, which I think certainly will come in the next five to ten years, which could coincide with the earth being taken over by Satan. But who knows.

"Let's face it. The last 36 years we've had UFO sightings. They're right here now, so it's just about ready to happen, I think. They're obviously watching us now. Otherwise, it's gonna be bombs from Russia or arrows from the east. One clairvoyant actually said that about 15 years from now fiery arrows would come from the east. It was Edgar Cayce, maybe. But he predicted the earthquake in California that didn't happen…"

Ship to ground! We've lost control of the interview! Ritchie Blackmore obviously displayed a great deal of himself in this interview, and I'm not gonna be dumb enough to try and summarise him with some slick closing remark. He may have said the most about himself when discussing his reputation as a heavy.

"I have a bad reputation but I don't mind. My good friends, people who really know me, know what I am." He said he got his image "by being very moody, being very sincere, telling people to fuck off when I shouldn't have done. But I don't care, not at all. I quite like it."

And that's the way it is. This is Jon Young, signing off from Connecticut, USA.

Interview with Roger Glover

Hank Bordowitz, Unpublished, March 1986 *(© Hank Bordowitz, 1986)*

Rainbow was dead. There was no doubt about that… Rainbow was dead as a doornail. Yet here I was, two years after the register of the band's burial had been signed by the clergyman, the clerk, the undertaker and the chief mourner. And here I faced the chief mourner himself, Roger Glover, to talk about a new Rainbow album, an odds and sods collection of mostly live tracks, appropriately dubbed Final Vinyl. Before us sits a bottle of Stolichnaya and a carton of Tropicana and by the end of the afternoon I was to learn that Roger Glover treated screwdrivers the way most diners dispense coffee – the never empty cup. In a way it was almost as much a metaphor for the album as the opening bit of Dickens was for the band.

The new album is called FINAL VINYL. That means that Rainbow is no more?

"Not as far as I know."

Why did they disband?

"Basically, Rainbow is Ritchie's vehicle. It was his band right from the start. He started it and he was the leader of it. I joined in 1979, and although it was still Ritchie's band, I was, I suppose, a fairly big part of Rainbow. When the Deep Purple reunion came about, there was no way we could pursue two different bands, two separate careers, so Rainbow had to cease in order to make way for Deep Purple. Whether or not, at some future time, Ritchie may decide to form another incarnation of Rainbow, that's entirely up to him."

It would have been too hard to keep both going?

"Ridiculous would be the word. Impossible would be another word."

You produced the new LP. Tell me about putting it together. Is it all stuff that you're on?

"Ronnie's stuff, 1978, that's Bob Daisley playing bass. I searched, I wanted to come out with an album that

Photo: Pictorial Press

spanned more of the time that Rainbow was in existence. Rainbow started in '75 I think, at least '76. The earliest recording I could come up with was '78 on our shelves. There may be some other recordings somewhere, but I couldn't search them out, and neither could our office, which is a shame because I wanted to find some early, vintage Rainbow.

Do you enjoy producing records? Have you produced anyone other than Rainbow?

"All of the Rainbow I worked on in the band I also produced. I used to do production. I would like to produce other people.

Could you see yourself making a career change?

"I don't think I would like to be a full time producer in this business. I'm much more at home being a writer and artist and have fun performing. I like to produce, but I don't think I'd like to be strictly a producer without being a performer, no. I did that for six years after I left Purple, I became a producer. I produced tons of different groups. I produced Rory Gallager, Nazareth, Judas Priest, David Coverdale, Michael Schenker, Elf, I did three albums with Elf, Ronnie Dio. I produced Barbie Benton at one point. I was a producer, a full time producer. I would produce anything that came my way.

How long did it take to put the LP together?

"About a month. Actually, listening itself, I spent three or four days listening to tapes before I made any decisions. Then I compiled my notes. I tried to figure out if we had enough material for an album. There were some performances I didn't like very much. In fact, initially, I was very doubtful whether it was even worth bothering with this. First of all, Rainbow's been finished two years. I'm fully involved in Deep Purple now. It's very exciting, I love it.

"And doing a project for my old band was really tedious. But the more I got into it, the more I listened to it, the more memories it brought back, the more I thought that, for Rainbow fans – and I'm not sure this album is going to set the world alight, but for Rainbow fans – it's a really interesting piece, because it does span six years of the band's history, and there are some older recordings, some classic recordings from Ronnie and Graham. I though it was a valid album to put out. It's a live album, with a few odd studio pieces that never really saw the light of day. Rather then just watching them gather dust on a shelf, I saw no reason why they shouldn't be out for the people to listen to and maybe get some enjoyment out of.

Now you and Ritchie were both with the band when Jon Lord took Deep Purple through their mercifully brief classical/orchestral period with Concerto for Group and Orchestra with the London

Philharmonic. You revisited using an orchestra for the Budakon recording on this album. Was that a throwback or was there some other reason for doing it?

"I remember that (the Jon Lord piece with the Royal Philharmonic, 1969) with absolutely pure clarity for some reason. There's always been a classical bent to our work. I love classical music myself. I love it a lot. Jon Lord, I think, was much more of a classical person than Ritchie was, although Ritchie had classical training, he very quickly left that and was into the blues and rock and, I think, returned to classical music somewhat later in his career.

"The early days of Rainbow, I think the classical started coming out, much more than it had in the original Deep Purple. I think the classical influence in Deep Purple was much more Jon Lord than Ritchie. But Ritchie now, and in the last six, seven years, has let the classical side of him show through. Ritchie had been wanting to do a gig with an orchestra for a long time, in a much more rock way. He didn't want to repeat the Deep Purple thing.

"The Deep Purple thing was really a concerto for group and orchestra. It was really a piece of classical music with a group in it. I think Ritchie's idea was the other way around. He wanted the group, but the orchestral type addition to enhance the rock part, not the other way around. We had no idea that this was going to be the last gig that Rainbow ever did. The decision to do Deep Purple hadn't fully been made at the point we went to Japan. But Ritchie, previous to any Deep Purple reunion ideas, had said let's get an orchestra to do it, and the manager had looked into it and found a way to get an orchestra for two days. Only two, because it's so expensive to do.

"Even just a string orchestra, it's a hefty thing. We arranged to do it in Japan, because the Japanese side of it said they'd pay for it as long as they could film it. This is how deals are done. So we went there, and it was a wonderful way for Rainbow to end.

"As I said, we didn't know it was going to be our last gig, but it was fortunate that it was recorded and the orchestra was there. It was a great way to bow out. It was touch and go. We weren't sure we could do it correctly, but it came off reasonably well. It could have been better, if we had more rehearsal time, etc, etc, but in the event, the way that it was done was great because there was no announcement made that it was going to be anything special, anything other than a Rainbow hard rock show. And we were in the Budokan and the crowd was there. It was a normal rock show for about an hour. Then Ritchie started to play the opening strains to Difficult to Cure, Beethoven's Ninth, and the curtains backstage opened, and there was this orchestra, bathed in rainbow light. It was a great moment. You could hear the audience gasp. What a great feeling that was! It was a great feeling. And it's not something I think we should repeat. Certainly it's not something you can go on the road with, but every now and again, for a special occasion like that, it's great. And the fact that it was recorded, and it's part of the video, it was a nice touch.

Rock 'n' roll should have the capacity to surprise its audience.

"That's very important."

I understand that Blackmore is a tough guy to work with...

"That's true to a certain extent. His reputation is not built on nothing. It's a little misguided at times. He is difficult at times, but at times he's not that difficult, he's very easy to work with. I've had a hard time working with him sometimes. He has his vision of what he wants to do, and sometimes he has a hard way of communicating to other people. Now, I know him really well, so I find it much easier to work with him than other people. But I don't think he's difficult for the sake of being difficult. I think he's as much a perfectionist as I am in a different way. I am just as much a perfectionist when it comes to getting studios and stuff like that, I really try for the very best. And he does, too. I think it's only when he comes up against people who don't play the way he wants them to play, or are maybe taking a bit of a passenger seat in whatever vehicle Ritchie happens to be on, or people who don't care about the music as much as Ritchie cares about it. When that happens, you see a side of Ritchie that most people give him the reputation for. They get fired, he gets angry, he gets pissed off, and when Ritchie gets pissed off with you, you know it! There's no way you're not going to know it. He gets into a real black mood. But that's because you're not toeing the line, you're not pulling your weight.

"Ritchie, if nothing else, is a hard worker. He works hard. He practises every day. If he can't get a part right, he'll work it and work it, and he can't stand to see sloppy musicianship. And there's loads of sloppy musicianship around. So a lot of his reputation stems from that. I think he is a moody guy, I think he's also a brilliant guitarist. So I put up with his moods, because what he gives the world is much better than the negative side that his moods create. I'm moody as well, it's just that he's got the reputation for it.

So now that Rainbow is no more, what's going on with Deep Purple?

"We've had a writing session. Before Christmas we all got together and rehearsed and stuff. We've got some great ideas. And we're looking for a place to record. We're hoping to start in early April.

How has Deep Purple changed in the ten years since Blackmore split?

"That's an enormous question. I think we have a new found awareness of each other that we didn't have before. I think before we were a band that really didn't know what we were doing. We worked and worked and worked, and that was probably the ultimate reason for the demise of the band, was that we worked too hard. We burned ourselves out very quickly. And also we achieved an awful lot of success and it's very difficult for that not to change you. I think some of us were changed by that, and that led to a few more personal differences.

"Eleven years down the line, we've been apart for eleven years, at least we were in 1984 when we got back together again, I think obviously with the passing of years, you get maturity, and you get a different view of the world. You're basically the same person, you play the same kind of instrument, you think more or less the same kind of thoughts. I don't think people change that much, but I think right now we have a lot more respect for each other than we did in the early days. So I think that's what enabled us to reform, and not just reform, but regenerate, recreate. I think we're much more excited about being together and playing together, and really feel like we belong together, than we did in the early days. In the early days it felt like such a big accident, we were thrown together, and suddenly, boom! We've got a platinum album.

Everything happened so quickly. Now we've got it much more in perspective.

Before Deep Purple started dabbling in progressive rock, before you became a hard rock band, you were covering Joe South tunes. It was kind of like the Moody Blues, you were really an R&B roots group.

"Purple, originally, in 1968, was started by the drummer of the Searchers, funnily enough, who then went mad and knocked it out. Chris Curtis was his name. But it left Ritchie and Jon and the management, and they got this group together, and I think the early Deep Purple was much more known for its extravagant arrangements of other people's songs than it was for original material, though they did write some original material, a couple of good songs. But by far, the best point of the band was the grandiose arrangements of other people's songs: River Deep, Mountain High, Hush, Kentucky Woman, etc.

"That only happened for about 18 months, they did a couple of tours and obviously that was going nowhere. They needed original material that was good. When they did a reshuffle, Ian Gillan and I had been a songwriting partnership before that for years in our own band. When we joined Purple, the songwriting really took over. We didn't do anyone else's material after that, we did purely our own material.

"What we're doing now is getting ready for an album. We haven't got anything to talk about in terms of an album. And this is a Rainbow thing, even though Rainbow is dead and gone two years ago. That's why I'm

here.

How intense was it, going on the road with Deep Purple after all those years apart?

"It wasn't intense, actually. It was very enjoyable. We just had a lark. We just had good fun, and after all, there is nothing wrong with that. If you're satisfied and happy and relaxed you're making good music. I think it all comes out in the music. It all comes out in the ideas. If you're unhappy about something, your ideas aren't that strong. It speaks for itself. It was a great experience. Getting back on the road again after six years as a producer was great. My first date with Rainbow in 1979, that was so much an uplift, it was fabulous to be back onstage. The Purple thing was not that traumatic an occasion, because we had all been working solidly for the last 11 years. Every single one of us had been touring. Ian Gillan had his own band, did no less than 200 dates a year for four, five years. It's not as if we all came out of retirement.

Renaissance Rebirth

Joel McIver, Acoustic magazine, December 2004 *(© Joel McIver 2004)*

For three decades he played riff-heavy music with the seminal rock band Deep Purple. Then he discovered 500-year-old music which changed his life (and trousers) forever. Joel McIver meets the acoustic scene's most unlikely figurehead, Ritchie Blackmore.

Few musicians possess an aura of mystery as impenetrable as that of legendary guitarist Ritchie Blackmore, whose distinguished career has seen him compose some of the most enduring riffs in history (even tribes people in the depths of the Amazon jungle can hum the main riff to Smoke on the Water), scale the rock pantheon and retreat in recent years to the stubbornly niche area of traditional Renaissance music.

His CV is intimidating: he started life as a session player and then co-founded Deep Purple in 1968. After knocking out a clutch of classic rock albums including The Book of Taliesyn (1969), Concerto for Group and

Orchestra (1970), Fireball (1971), Machine Head (1972), Burn (1974), and Stormbringer (1974), he left the Purps in April 1975. Rumour has it that his mercurial, almost lordly, nature had led to dissent in the Purple camp, although he has rarely commented on the subject.

He then formed Ritchie Blackmore's Rainbow, through which a veritable who's-who of rock passed (Ronnie James Dio, Jim Bain, Cozy Powell, Purple bassist Roger Glover, Don Airey, Graham Bonnet) and which made him one of this country's most important rock icons. Admit it, you've hummed along with Since You Been Gone at some point – we all have.

An 11-year sojourn in the reformed Purple between 1984 and 1995 left him tired of rock and its attendant demands, however, and when he resurfaced in 1997 with a new outfit called Blackmore's Night, no one knew what to expect.

What we got was a remarkable band centring on Blackmore, now playing a variety of classical instruments (many of ancient design) alongside his wife Candice Night. Their music, far from being a rock-mongous blend of riffs and percussion as in his previous bands, was mainly subtle acoustic classical-folk of obscure European origin. A cult movement has grown up around the band and the wider Renaissance scene, largely in Germany, where the band have even done 'castle tours' for that genuinely medieval vibe.

Blackmore seems to have found his place at last – he even dresses like a man born half a millennium ago. When Acoustic spoke to him for the hallowed spot of front cover star of issue No. 1, we were uncertain what to expect. In fact, Blackmore turned out be a humble, relaxed and self-deprecating kind of chap: can this really be the much-feared rock overlord of old? Let's investigate…

Ritchie, for 30 years you were a rock god. What got you into playing mellow acoustic music?

What spurred me on was seeing a band in Germany back in 1985 and thinking, I have to do this. It moved me so much, I had to do it. And the better we get at it, the more bands there are cropping up doing Renaissance music. There are now 100 bands doing this in Germany. It's like a rekindling of the old music.

There was a Renaissance music scene in Europe ages before you showed up with Blackmore's Night. What do the established players say when they're asked to play with you, a so-called rock performer?

There's an incredible snobbery in this scene! They don't lighten up. On the other hand, I know people who play Renaissance music and can't stand it any more and want to be in a rock band. It works both ways. If you're not playing it exactly the way it says on the score, you should be excommunicated!

Do you get Deep Purple and Rainbow fans at Blackmore's Night shows?

It's a bit of both. We seem to have acquired a whole new audience, made up of Purple and Rainbow fans from the old days. It's about 60-40 per cent old and new fans, which is quite gratifying. I'm getting older and the fans are getting older, and I think their taste changes too, so they're not into hard rock quite as much any more. We do two or three hours and I play electro-acoustic guitars. We incorporate that at the end of the show as it's an electric and acoustic tour: the last half hour is all electric rock tunes, really. Rock versions of what we do.

What instruments do you use?

Unfortunately, I have about ten guitars on stage with me for every song. I have these guitars made for me by a Japanese guy called Kawakami, who used to be with Yari-Alvarez, but has now left and only does personal guitars, I think. He never accepts any money for the guitars he makes for me! He's made me three guitars based on designs which I draw for him. They're all single-cutaway designs, but the latest one has a lute on the top. They have piezo pickups under the bridge. Sometimes I use a Roland synthesiser which is incorporated into the guitar, with the controls all on the back so it doesn't take away from the acoustic look.

Do you get a decent acoustic sound out of the electro-acoustic instruments, or do they have to amplified?

Well, the bodies are only about two inches wide, so they're very quiet, obviously, and suit the electric environment more than the acoustic one. I only use them onstage: when I'm offstage I use different acoustics. I also use a Fender Telecaster electro-acoustic: I think they only made about eight of them! I showed them to the guys at Fender the other day and they didn't know anything about it, even though it was only made about eight years ago. I think they just made a few and then got confused and went on to other stuff. It's an incredibly good guitar, though, with a very thin neck, which I like. It's just like an electric Tele except it's got F-holes, although it sounds nothing like an electric.

I sometimes also use a Godin guitar, which has very responsive pickups. I like the slider controls, they're handy when you're playing a solo onstage – you don't have to grapple for the knob. It's just a normal guitar off the shelf, there's no custom modifications to it. I also use mandolas and bouzoukis, which I get from Fylde, the English maker. The first ones I got from them were just standard instruments so I could see what they were like, but I've just ordered a custom double-neck guitar.

Do you have a large guitar collection?

Not as big as people might think. I have about 16 guitars. I've offloaded quite a few over the years – I like to give them to people who don't have guitars. I remember the days when I couldn't afford a guitar and I wished

111

someone would give me one! I have quite a few Strats, most of which are stored under the stairs.

Do you still endorse Fender?

I do have an endorsement deal with Fender — I could bother them all the time and collect guitars, but I don't believe in that. I know some guitarists bleed the company dry, and go around to every guitar maker and say, 'Oh, I wanna play your guitar', when they have no intention of it. But I do have custom stuff made up for me sometimes. I had a custom 12-string acoustic made up for me, but I never played it. It doesn't sound right, which is the problem with custom instruments: even if it doesn't sound right you've still got to buy it and get on with it! I'm not a guitar maker, so there are things I don't know. But I love 12-string guitars, I have a Halo right here by my foot which I was just playing. I don't use them onstage, though, because of the feedback. I used to get feedback on stage when I first started, until I started using the very thin guitars. The only way around feedback for me, when I'm playing particular guitar pieces, is to turn the guitar way down. It's completely the opposite approach to the electric feedback effect, where you need a lot of sound.

With an acoustic, I believe that the quieter you are the better the sound is. Of course, when we're playing in front of a lot of people and I turn myself down, the sound guy tries to compensate and I tell him off. There's something about the acoustic that should be played quietly. It should not be cranked up like some kind of cheap electric.

Presumably the engineer could just turn up the house PA and leave the actual backline and monitors fairly low?

They do, but I also think that when people are seeing someone play an acoustic guitar, they should really listen. They should listen to the subtleties, rather than just have the performer trying to play over the local drunks by turning up the guitar! But luckily, among the people who turn up to see us, we rarely have people who are noisy.

Does the electro-acoustic show work better with smaller crowds than in a big arena?

You know, when you start getting over about 3,000 people, you can compensate with the PA – but generally, the more people you have in the audience, the less they're gonna listen. In a big crowd there are always people who come just because they want to have a party, which is fine if you're playing loud, but if you're playing quiet like me, it can come unstuck sometimes.

What amps do you use?

I use two amps on stage – a Trace Elliot, and out of the back of that a Fender Acoustasonic, which is a great amp for acoustics. I really like them, although they're quite expensive. They give this kind of stereo effect, almost like a moving-speaker effect. I don't use pedals, because if I use too many effects things usually go wrong onstage! I always try to keep it as simple as possible.

What was your first guitar?

A Framus acoustic, for seven guineas, in 1925 I think… no, this would be 1957, when I was 11 or 12. I bought it in Hounslow. My first electric guitar was a Höfner Club 50. I loved Club 50s but I never see them advertised, ever. I wouldn't mind buying one if I ever saw one. No, I never look at eBay, it's one of those things that I think about but I never pursue. A bit like a Gretsch Jet Firebird — Candice said, I'll buy you one for your birthday, and I said no, there has to be something I don't have that I want.

That used to be the ultimate guitar for me. I remember going into Jim Marshall's shop in Ealing – Mitch Mitchell was working behind the counter! – before he made amplifiers. I went in with the intention of buying a Jet Firebird and I came out with a Gibson 335 because the guy in the shop told me that was a much better guitar. He said I'd thank him sometime for it… I was quite bewildered. I came out thinking, why am I holding a Gibson when I wanted that Gretsch? But in actual fact it was a better guitar. He was one of these purist jazz players, you know. And ever since then I keep looking at them and thinking, God they look so good.

What instruments do you use when you're just jamming offstage?

Usually Lakewood acoustics. We were touring in Germany once and this guy gave me one and I kept it. I didn't play it for months, and then suddenly I remembered it. It's made of Brazilian wood, I think, and it resonates very well. So I had three guitars custom-made by them, including a lute-guitar which I had made up. It looks just like a lute but it was a 12-string guitar. Then the neck got broken by somebody who dropped it onstage and wouldn't own up… after it was fixed the 12-strings didn't work, so I just use it as a 6-string.

Do you experiment with tunings

Just a little bit. But I'm still having trouble with the orthodox tuning! I quite often use a drop-D, but I don't go for fancy non-standard tunings very often. I do experiment with the bouzoukis and the mandolas a bit, I tune them in fifths instead of fourths.

Who are your favourite guitar players?

My favourite acoustic guitarist is probably Gordon Giltrap. Also John Renbourn, who is excellent. I saw him play the other day, he came out and grunted at the audience and got on with it without any showbiz at all. Absolutely excellent! But when I started playing guitar, the people you listened to were the Hank Marvins and

Django Reinhardts of this world. I also went through a Wes Montgomery period of about six months. Les Paul and Chet Atkins were heroes of mine too.

What about the Delta and Chicago blues players?

I was never a big blues fan. I liked BB King, but I was either more into pop or classical. I like to play the blues now and again, but I find it a little bit limiting. I loved some of Eric Clapton's stuff with Cream – I think the solo on I Feel Free is brilliant – but other than him I just didn't get it. Although with Hendrix I could see what the fuss was about. Then again, he would have made it had he not even played the guitar, I think – he just had that ambience around him. The man was from the moon.

And the folkies?

Bob Dylan is my hero, but not because of his guitar playing. There's just something about him that hits the soul when he's singing. Candice can't figure out what the hell I see in him.

So how did the classical influences, which have come to the fore with Blackmore's Night, come about?

When I started the guitar, my father insisted I learn to read music and play classical stuff by Segovia and Bach, which I failed miserably at. But the melodies and the discipline stuck with me, and once I'd got the feeling of the guitar I went back into that area. Not as a purist, though: I couldn't really sit down to play, and I'd forgotten how to read music. I couldn't play the preludes and things any more, but they were still there, at the back of my subconscious, I think. I was never a particularly good pupil at school.

Has your grasp of classical music theory been useful?

Well, I do a lot of guesswork. I love listening to classical and Renaissance music, so I don't approach it from an academic point of view – I come to it by ear, so to speak. When I studied Bach, I thought that some of his organ works related to the guitar very well: they had that sort of power. Some of his work had incredible trills in it which bothered me at the time: a bit like playing an F major for the first time, which took me six months! Every time I got to an F when I was playing I had to stop, and the teacher said, 'Don't worry, you'll get it'. Any bar chord I did was just a clonk.

Studying classical guitar must have been good for your plucking-hand technique?

That's right. I've changed my style a lot over the last ten years, because it was all playing with a pick before that and the Renaissance stuff is all fingerpicking. Now I have to grow my nails, which is a whole headache, because they always break just before a show, and I can't put on fingerpicks because I always find them too bulky. Luckily, Candice showed me these things called acrylics which you paint on your nails. It's quite smelly stuff but it works. It's amazing how important the nails are, because if I break a nail all you can hear is the fingertip. I didn't realise that nails were such high maintenance!

You're based in America. How do they take to Renaissance music?

Well, over here they only really know about rock and jazz and blues. There are only one or two bands over here, like the Terranova Consort, who play this kind of music, so to find the music you have to go to the back of the record store to the part marked 'throwaway items'! Luckily, I know what to look for because I know the instruments that are being played. They have crumhorns and shawms and hurdy-gurdies... now that's an instrument. I have two hurdy-gurdies. Do you know what they are?

That's where you turn the handle, right?

And the monkey jumps up and down, yes! That's the instrument I'd play if I didn't play the guitar. It's great. I'm still a novice, though. I play it through an amp onstage and it sounds unbelievable: I think if the rock 'n' roll 18-year-olds of today heard a hurdy-gurdy played properly through an amp, with some echo, they'd probably buy that instead of a guitar. It has even more of a roar than a guitar. It has amazing sustain and it sounds like an elephant. But they don't look cool and they're not the 'in' thing to play, so you never hear them. You have to turn the handle like an old woman.

Anyway, I live in America but in England it's also difficult to perform this kind of music. They don't understand why a rock performer would want to play to 500 or 1,000 people in a castle when I should be in a rock band playing to 50,000. We've spoken about doing the festival circuit but, again, there are a lot of closed doors there and a lot of political stuff with the folkies. Ian Anderson of Jethro Tull said once that he had the same problem: because he played some rock, he encountered some snobbery. I thought that was ridiculous!

Would you like Renaissance music to become more popular, or would you like it to remain in its niche?

Good point, I've often thought about this. I have a bad habit of liking anything that other people don't. If it was extremely popular I don't know if I'd like it so much. There's something about the unattainable and the hidden that turns me on.

Maybe the gothic-rock kids into Evanescence and Nightwish would get into it if they were exposed to it.

It does border on that. The guys in Nightwish are friends with Candice and they do similar music sometimes. They add more of a rock thing to it though.

Are you still in touch with the other Deep Purple guys?

I'm in touch with Jon Lord, yes. Tell him it's his turn to buy dinner. I bought it last time!